A Design for a Model College Financial Aid Office

by **William D. Van Dusen**
Educational Consultant
Brookdale, California

John J. O'Hearne
Director, New England Regional Office
The College Board

Revised 1980 by
William D. Van Dusen

P9-AOQ-628

College Entrance Examination Board, New York, 1980

Copies of this publication may be ordered from College Board Publication Orders, Box 2815, Princeton, New Jersey 08541. The price is $6.25.

Inquiries regarding this publication should be addressed to Editorial Office, The College Board, 888 Seventh Avenue, New York, New York 10019.

Contents

Acknowledgment

Some of the material in this publication first appeared in a report entitled *An Idealization of a Collegiate Financial Aid Office*, completed as the first part of a three-volume study funded by a research grant from the Coordinating Board, Texas College and University System to the College Board. With the approval of the Coordinating Board, the report was reissued in 1968 by the College Board under the title *Design for a Model College Financial Aid Office*. A second edition of the publication with revisions by William D. Van Dusen was published in 1973.

Although this publication is based on earlier work, changes in college student financial aid called for more substantive revisions than simply modifying data from 1968 and 1973 to reflect current conditions. This third edition substantially modifies material presented previously and includes much new information.

Introduction

Programs of financial assistance to students attending post-secondary institutions of education in the United States have changed drastically since 1643, when Lady Anne Mowlson gave 100 English pounds to "constitute an endowment for the support at Harvard of 'some poore schooler'" and thereby established the first recorded scholarship program in the United States.[1]

That sentence introduced the first and second editions of the College Scholarship Service's *Design for a Model College Financial Aid Office*, and provided an historical benchmark against which the then-current considerations of the "ideal" office could be measured. The first edition appeared in 1968, 10 years after the modern entry of the federal government into the provision of aid to undergraduate students with the establishment of the National Defense (now Direct) Student Loan (NDSL) Program. It was the NDSL program that created, for most institutions, the need to establish specific offices responsible for aid administration and to appoint individuals with titles like "director of financial aid."

The second edition appeared in 1973, just after the federal government had embarked upon another major expansion of undergraduate student aid through passage of the Basic Educational Opportunity Grant (BEOG) Program, the "foundation" upon which it was intended all other federal, state, institutional, and private student aid would rest. The great expansion of federal efforts in the area of student aid reflected by the Basic Grant program caused the aggregate assistance estimated to be available for the 1973–74 academic year to have grown to more than $4 billion from the approximately $600 million estimated to have been available in 1969–70.

This third edition appears on the eve of another great expansion in the federal student aid effort. The Middle Income Student Assistance Act (MISAA) of 1978 (Public Law 95–566) greatly expands eligibility for participation in the Basic Grant program and provides federal guarantees and interest subsidies for substantially all loans made by commercial lending institutions to students participating in postsecondary education or to their parents. The American Council on Education estimates that the direct federal student aid available for the 1979–80 academic year will total nearly $6.7 billion (see Table 1).[2]

Table 1. Estimated Program Levels, Federal Student Aid, 1979–80

	Millions
Basic Educational Opportunity Grants	$2,444
Supplemental Educational Opportunity Grants	340
College Work-Study Program	550
National Direct Student Loans	640
State Student Incentive Grants	77
Guaranteed Student Loans	2,636
Total	$6,687

If these programs of direct student aid are added to other forms of federal assistance to students enrolled in postsecondary education (tax expenditures, GI Bill educational benefits, and social security student benefits), the total federal investment in aid to students probably exceeds $12.3 billion.[3]

State efforts in support of student aid have also increased markedly. In the 1969–70 academic year the total of state scholarship and grant expenditures was estimated to be $240 million. For the 1978–79 academic year the National Association of State Scholarship and Grant Programs (NASSGP) estimates that $828.9 million will be provided by state governments (including the federal government's contribution to the State Student Incentive Grant Program).[4]

Information about institutional and private contributions to student aid programs is more difficult to obtain, but the most commonly accepted estimates say that these sources provide about $1 billion per year. Taken together, the federal, state, institutional, and private efforts to aid students participating in postsecondary education in the United States will probably exceed $8.5 billion in direct assistance and would clearly exceed $14 billion if the indirect federal subsidies mentioned earlier were included. Estimates of the number of students served by those programs suggest that as many as 75 percent of the enrolled undergraduate students qualify for assistance.

In the midst of all those impressive numbers, it is important to remember that the central role of student aid is to assist students as individuals. Joseph P. Cangemi has observed that "the student as a human being seems not to be an important concept in far too many institutions of higher education but rather seems more appreciated as a statistic: a degree aspirant, a major, a minor, a female, a datum to report for state financial support, possessor of a good I.Q., a genius, a potential member of a discipline, among other things. In short, in too many institutions of higher learning the student is perceived as an entity, a thing, something to feed intellectually and to obtain back from in return conditioned regurgitated feedback, or to use as an appropriate statistic for the benefit of the institution or the state."[5]

Applying that concern to financial aid, Robert E. Stoltz commented that the job of financial aid administrator "may become more clerk-like in character, or the financial aid administrator can emerge as a student-oriented counselor, assisting the prospective and present student in coping with his full array of financial concerns . . . the future will require . . . being aware of and concerned with the basic problem of what education in this society is all about."[6]

The purpose of this booklet is not to provide a "how-to-do-it" guide to the day-to-day administration of the financial aid office on individual campuses, but rather to suggest some of the general philosophical considerations that should be part of a concern for a "more than clerkly" function. It is intended not only for aid officers but also for other administrators on and off the campus concerned with the development of financial aid programs, for students interested in pursuing careers in higher educational administration, and for concerned private individuals interested in knowing how this enterprise is managed. For as Stoltz continues, "Put bluntly, higher education in the 1970s and 1980s will probably be judged far more by the goodness of its managers than by the sophistication of its machines and the majesty of its masonry."

In the preparation of the first two editions of this booklet, much of the supportive information was obtained from an unpublished report of a survey of the financial aid policies, organization, and practices in accredited four-year institutions of higher learning conducted in the 1965–66 academic year by the Bureau of Applied Social Research of Columbia University for the College Board.[7] For this edition new information collected by the National Association of Student Financial Aid Administrators (NASFAA) in 1977 was available to provide some indications of the current state of operations and activities of the nation's financial aid offices.[8]

The NASFAA data includes responses from 1,912 individuals who were engaged in the administration of financial assistance programs in the fall of 1977. Half of those respondents were employed at independent private institutions, 42 percent at public institutions, and 8 percent at proprietary institutions. That distribution of respondents permits statements to be made about the first two types of institutions with relative confidence; statements about the proprietary institutions are based on a very small sample and should be considered at best tentative.

Although this booklet is not intended to describe the characteristics of the financial aid *professional* (the NASFAA publication does that very adequately), it is worth noting that a significant change appears to have taken place in that aspect of the administration of financial aid since the first two editions of this publication were prepared. In the 1960s and 70s, turnover among the aid office staff was an endemic problem. Many individuals would take jobs in aid and move out of them as quickly as possible — into other jobs in the institution or out of postsecondary education all together. The recent NASFAA survey, however, found that more than half of the respondents had six years' or more experience in aid. Even among the ranks of the counselors (who could be presumed to be the least experienced), fewer than 1 in 5 reported less than one year's experience in aid administration. Nearly 7 in 10 of the respondents agreed that financial aid was sufficiently satisfying to become a lifetime career.[9] Apparently a considerable level of stability has developed in the ranks of aid administrators. This stability and career-orientation should facilitate the further development of aid activities to promote the educational, social, personal, and financial growth of individuals participating in postsecondary education in the decade of the 80s.

What Constitutes Financial Aid to Students?

Development of Student Financial Aid Programs

Early programs of student financial aid were begun with money given to colleges by private individuals specifically to aid needy and worthy students; in many instances those funds were supplemented by allocations from the general funds of the institutions themselves. The purpose of student aid was to make a college education available to those individuals who could not themselves afford to pay the costs.

"The college was not to be an institution of narrow privilege. Society required the use of all its best talents, and while it would, of course, always be easier for a rich boy than a poor boy to go to college, persistence and ambition and talent were not to be denied. The American college, therefore, was an expression of Christian charity, both in the assistance that it gave to the needy young men and in the assistance that it received from affluent old men."[10]

As the term scholarship was used initially in connection with student financial aid, it meant a gift of money granted to a student who could not otherwise afford to attend college.

This original emphasis on student financial need continued through the years until the 1940s, although during this period of time many alterations and embellishments were made in practices followed by institutions in the administration of student aid programs. These alterations were made in an effort to serve national and institutional purposes by means of student financial aid while at the same time enabling needy students to attend college.

Shortly after the beginning of the twentieth century, state governments began to establish student aid programs to realize specific state objectives. Connecticut established a program in 1909 for reasons relating to personnel recruitment. New York established its Regents' Program shortly thereafter for general student assistance purposes, while Pennsylvania organized one to realize largely political purposes. By 1955 about half of the states had established some kind of program.

Institutions used aid funds to recruit students from special groups in the hope that the subsidized students would help to attract other enrollees who would be able to pay the charges. Colleges also desired to have some needy students on the campus so that they would not be characterized in the public's mind as snobbish havens for the affluent.[11] In addition, institutions of higher learning inaugurated special financial aid programs to recognize or to reward particularly outstanding skills developed by students in nonacademic or cocurricular areas; for example, grants were awarded to students for special ability in athletics, debating, music, and other fields.

The general continuation of emphasis on the financial need of the student as a criterion for assistance during those years was also evidenced by the establishment of textbook loans for needy students, the operation of special dining halls for the poor, and the introduction of manual labor programs for students. An early example of the poor being given first preference in locating term-time jobs was the establishment at Yale in 1900 of the "Bureau of Self Help" to assist needy but ambitious students.[12]

The desire to achieve a number of different goals by means of student financial aid continued to be apparent after the end of World War II. In the closing months of the war, the Servicemen's Readjustment Act of 1944, known familiarly as the GI Bill, was passed. This action by a grateful citizenry channeled into college large numbers of students who brought with them substantial amounts of support from the federal government granted without regard to financial need. Many institutions found that scholarship funds previously used to support needy students were no longer required for that purpose, and those colleges began to use these funds to attract and to reward students with academic or other special talents with little or no regard to their financial conditions. The term *scholarship* thus gained new meaning as a gift of money used to reward talented students, and the public became familiar with such phrases as *academic scholarship*, *athletic scholarship*, and *music scholarship*.

Yet another shift in the rationale of financial aid programs began in the late 1950s when additional agencies of the federal government began to provide large amounts of assistance to college students. The National Defense (Direct) Student Loan Program, authorized by the National Defense Education Act of 1958, was a major student financial aid effort by the federal government. The results of the NDSL program were dramatic, particularly in light of the fact that student loan programs had been available in some institutions since the early 1900s.[13] For example, it was estimated that prior to initiation of the NDSL program, $26 million was available in college loan programs, but only 50 percent of such funds was actually on loan. While those data might have seemed to indicate a reluctance on the part of students and their parents to borrow for educational expenses, the NDSL program in its first full year of operation advanced more than $60 million to students.[14] Although the NDSL program was clearly a loan program, it followed the pattern established by many earlier scholarship programs in requiring that preference among needy students be given to those of exceptional promise who would enter such areas as mathematics, science, foreign languages, engineering, and education. (Preferential consideration for outstanding students preparing to enter those special areas is no longer required by the NDSL program, although favorable cancellations of repayment for graduates working in particular areas continues this initial pattern.)

In 1964 the Congress of the United States passed the Economic Opportunity Act, which among its provisions authorized the establishment of the College Work-Study Program. This program combines federal, institutional, and private funds to encourage and to extend the employment of students, both on the campus and in nonprofit off-campus agencies. Postsecondary educational institutions that participate in the College

Work-Study Program are required to maintain, from their own funds, their previous level of student employment unless they receive a waiver for good cause. This program is intended to assist and to advance, but not to replace, the efforts of the colleges to provide jobs for students. Initially the College Work-Study Program was restricted to students from extremely low-income families. These severe limitations have since been revised, and now it is required only that preference in employment be given to students from low-income families.

The Higher Education Act of 1965 centralized the administration of sponsored student aid activities in the United States Office of Education and established the Educational Opportunity Grants Program (now the Supplemental Educational Opportunity Grants Program). This program authorizes direct grants, that are not repaid, to students who demonstrate that they and their families are unable to pay for higher education. The grants may not exceed $1,500 or one-half the amount the student needs to go to college, whichever is less, and a matching amount must be made available to the student from other approved sources of student financial aid.

The trend toward increased federal involvement in providing financial assistance to college students was continued with the establishment of the Federally Insured (Guaranteed) Student Loan Program, the State Student Incentive Grants Program, special grant and loans programs specifically for law-enforcement officers, nurses, and doctors; the extension of social security benefits to age 22 for recipients who are enrolled in postsecondary institutions; and the inclusion of provisions for grant assistance in such programs as the Model Cities Development Act. But it was establishment of the Basic Educational Opportunity Grants in the Education Amendments of 1972 that provided the next massive attempt of the federal government to provide broad-based support for students in postsecondary education.

As initially enacted, Basic Grants were intended to be an "entitlement" assuring that up to $1,400 per year in gift assistance would be available to any student who, "for lack of such a grant, would be unable to obtain the benefits of a post-secondary education."[15] Low levels of funding during the early years of the program hampered its ability to provide that complete entitlement. However, the support of the Administration for passage of the Middle Income Student Assistance Act (MISAA) in 1978 and for the appropriations necessary to actually fund the grants provided by MISAA makes it appear that the full entitlement will be available to undergraduate students for the 1979–80 academic year.

The major federal programs of student aid have now departed from an earlier practice of limiting eligibility to academically superior students and stipulate only that the student maintain normal progress toward a degree according to the standards usually used by the institution to define "normal progress." The essential criterion of these current federal programs is the student's need for funds. Thus, the purpose of the principal financial aid programs of today is markedly similar to the original intention of student aid programs—to make the best use of the talents of all the country's young men and women.[16]

The entitlement concept of the Basic Educational Opportunity Grants (also partially a characteristic of the Federally Insured [Guaranteed] Loan Program) represents another shift in the focus of the major federal student aid programs. Under this concept, any student planning enrollment in any postsecondary institution is theoretically assured of a certain amount of support. In effect, these programs provide a guarantee of aid whenever the basic eligibility criteria are met. Theoretically, the only role that the postsecondary institutions play in the delivery of these programs is to certify that the student is in fact enrolled and to provide information about costs so that an award amount can be calculated.

While the federal student aid programs have been moving away from any involvement of academic achievement, some institutions have been moving toward "no-need" scholarships as an inducement to students. A survey conducted by the College Board in 1977 found that 71 percent of responding institutions were granting no-need/merit awards, a sharp increase over the 54 percent found in a 1975 survey.[17] This practice appears to be provoked by a fear of falling enrollments: "since the traditional pool for postsecondary education will soon decline, barring special efforts colleges will be unable to enroll as many students as they now enroll. This fact, along with a sudden energy-based increase in operating costs, has elicited from colleges a variety of reactions: services for nontraditional students, grantsmanship, aggressive recruiting, advertising, and surely not least programs offering students financial aid as an inducement to attend."[18] This even though the College Board survey showed that only 17.7 percent of the responding institutions indicated that they had done any systematic studies of those who accepted or refused no-need awards.[19]

Current Forms of College Student Financial Aid

In the most general sense financial aid for students attending postsecondary educational institutions may be described as any means available to offset or diminish the expenses normally incurred by an individual while attending college. Typically, however, a more limited view is taken: student financial aid is considered to be only those expense-reducing means (money, goods, or services) awarded directly to or for a student and used to defray educational and living expenses as contrasted with an award made directly to a postsecondary institution to assist it in meeting operating expenses. For example, an award by a donor to a student to meet the expenses of room and board is classified as student aid, but a bequest from the same donor to a college to enable it to maintain low-cost housing for students is not so categorized.

Student financial aid programs may be generally organized into three categories: grants, loans, and jobs. These three categories may be further subdivided according to the special characteristics of individual programs. The first major subdivision of each of the three general classes of aid is made in terms of whether or not applicants and their families must submit financial data to show a need for assistance, and whether or not the amount of aid to be awarded is related to need for funds to meet educational expenses.

Grants

Scholarships or *grants-in-aid* are awards of money, tuition discounts, remission of tuition and fees, or similar considerations that require neither repayment nor specific service to be performed by the student. Frequently they are made to further a particular institutional purpose such as increased enrollment of students from specific ethnic, social, economic, or geographic segments of the population.

Service awards are similar to scholarships and grants, except that these are awarded in return for specific services rendered to the institution and are usually made in recognition of unusual ability in areas such as athletics, debating, or music. Service awards differ from employment because they are generally grants of money and not payment for work on an hourly basis or on the basis of completion of specific tasks. The term *grants* is used here to include forms of gift aid.

The vast majority of grant assistance currently available is provided by the state and federal governments through programs administered according to specific procedures and under what are frequently seen as rigid rules and regulations. There frequently appear circumstances where the particular rules and regulations governing the administration of a federal or state grant program may technically disqualify an applicant who, in the judgment of the financial aid administrator, should receive grant aid. It is, therefore, necessary to have additional funds available from institutional or private sources in order to be able to extend a grant to a student who technically is not qualified for assistance within the confines of a federal or state program.

Although there is pressure for colleges to limit awards of grant aid to students who have financial need, the data reported by Sidar and Potter indicate that institutions are increasingly using their own resources to recruit the academically talented with "no-need" scholarships while they use public money to recruit the financially disadvantaged with need-based offers of assistance. Some of these "no-need" programs reflect the traditional and historical connotations attached to the term "scholarship." Examples of such programs would include awards to relatives of benefactors of the institution; to residents of the community in which the institution is located; by denominational institutions to members of certain churches; and to students who plan to study in particular disciplines that are of limited popularity. Other programs reflect the concerns of institutions for enrollment of more students who can pay at least part of the bill from their own or their families' resources. It is this latter kind of concern that prompted participants in a recent conference on student aid policy to warn that "there is a real possibility of loss of public confidence in a system that stimulates increases in public appropriations for need-based programs and, at the same time, permits increases in institutional and private programs supporting no-need awards."[20]

Institutions of higher learning are frequently asked to administer funds on behalf of donors or sponsors who wish to select the recipient themselves, such as a local school Parent-Teacher Association, a community service club, or a fraternal organization on or off the campus, but who wish to disburse the money through the college. Such "trusteeship" accounts can provide substantial sums of assistance although they may not be considered a formal part of the financial aid program of the institution.

Loans

Loans are sums of money offered with the requirement that they be repaid in whole or in part, with or without the payment of interest. Applications for loan assistance may or may not call for the applicant and his family to report financial data in order to show a need for funds, and the amount loaned may or may not be contingent upon the amount of need. Some loan programs call for the payment of interest during the period of study, while others defer interest until after the student leaves college. While the definition of student financial aid given at the beginning of this section would seem to include all loans, loans as financial aid are generally considered to be only those made at a true rate of interest not greater than the prevailing rate for consumer credit. While commercial loans with a higher rate of interest may be used to defer payment of some educational expenses, they are usually not considered to be student financial aid in the customary sense of that term. (On the basis of a set of standardized definitions developed by Rauh,[21] the first edition of this publication asserted that no loan with a true interest rate of more than 6 percent would be considered as student aid — another example of the changes that have occurred in the past 15 years.)

Another kind of financial aid loan that has been discussed, but is not yet commonly available, is the "parent loan." This kind of program would provide federal insurance, guarantee, and possibly interest subsidy for loans made by commercial lending institutions to the parents of students participating in postsecondary education.[22] The amounts of these loans would reflect the portion of "expected parental contribution" that could not reasonably be met with current purchasing power (i.e., the part of the contribution reflecting the family's financial strength in asset holdings). Whether this kind of loan could be considered student financial aid is perhaps questionable, although it certainly would constitute aid for postsecondary study.

The major sources of loan funds are the federal and state governments, including those made by commercial lenders and subsidized under the Federally Insured (Guaranteed) Student Loan Program (which is the largest program currently in operation). Among the other large loan programs in the United

States are the National Direct Student Loan Program, the Health Professions Student Loan Program, and the Nursing Student Loan Program, all sponsored by the federal government.

In addition to loan funds provided by sources outside the institution, many colleges provide long-term and short-term loans to students from their own resources. Long-term, low-interest loans are repayable shortly after graduation or withdrawal although interest does not accrue as long as the student continues to be enrolled. Short-term or "petty cash" loan funds permit colleges to satisfy the emergency needs of students (for example, grocery or rent money until payday) in an efficient and economical manner. Typically these funds provide small amounts for a short period of time, such as "$30 for 30 days."

The importance of loans in a financial aid program, even at a low-cost publicly supported institution of higher learning, has increased as both the academic demands and the expenses of postsecondary education have become higher. It is increasingly difficult for students to support themselves (and in many cases their own families) through employment. Since grants seldom cover the entire cost of an educational program, loans become an important supplement. The difference between the need of the student and the funds that may be received in grants or provided through employment should be made available through loans.

Some student loan programs available from organizations and agencies other than the institutions of higher education do not require extensive on-campus administrative activity; for example, tuition loan programs available through commercial banks. The educational institution's involvement with such programs is minimal, frequently being limited to attesting to the lender that the applicant, or the applicant's child in the case of a loan to the parent, is a registered student and making some estimate of the educational expenses that may be incurred during the period of the loan. Other external loan programs, however, require that the institution provide an assessment of the student's financial need that may be as detailed as that done by the institution for its own programs.

Jobs

Some institutions consider student employment a form of financial aid only when the jobs are paid for from the funds of the college or from funds administered through the financial accounts of the institution. However, many institutions have broadened the meaning of employment as a form of aid to include all work opportunities for which the college assists in job placement or where the applicant receives preferential treatment because of his status as a student. For example, some colleges have standing agreements with certain local employers for placing a given number of students each semester in part-time jobs. Other institutions may have large cooperative educational programs that provide for employment one semester and study the next. The kinds of jobs that students can hold are limited only by the economic conditions in the campus community and the ingenuity and imagination of the financial aid administrator and the students. As with grants and loans, eligibility for employment and the amount of remuneration may or may not be determined on the basis of financial data from a student and family.

The duration of need-based employment typically is governed by the time required to earn a specific amount of money indicated as part of the financial aid award. If that duration does not correspond with the needs of the employer or the time required to complete a specific task, adjustments may need to be made in the other components of the student's aid package. Employment not based on financial need typically is not controlled either as to length of time or amount of earnings.

Many institutions make employment available to any student who wishes to work without regard to financial need. In those colleges, it is usually held that employment itself is an educational experience that will provide a worthwhile supplement to formal classroom instruction. Many institutions set aside a number of positions or a certain payroll dollar amount to be used for students who demonstrate financial need. Among such positions are term-time jobs assisting members of the faculty and administration, and service staffs; vacation employment; student agency arrangements (through which students operate service enterprises on the campus for profit); and what might be termed casual labor jobs (such as plant operations or work in a child-care center sponsored by the institution).

Principles and Practices
of Financial Aid Administration

Since the College Scholarship Service (CSS) was founded in 1954, it has become a generally accepted principle that financial aid should be awarded on the basis of financial need in order to enable the greatest number of students to begin or continue their educations and prepare for their roles in society. This principle is rooted in the knowledge that without such aid the equal participation in society of those from low-income families would be restricted. "When one is talking about financial aid, one is in reality speaking of access to higher education — who'll get in and who won't, who'll go to the quality schools and who won't, who'll be equipped to lead in the future and who'll be consigned to follow."[23]

In addition to that general principle, the following more specific statements were developed for and by the colleges, universities, scholarship agencies, secondary schools, and school systems that participate in the College Scholarship Service Assembly of the College Board. This statement of principles expresses a basic philosophy to which large numbers of institutions subscribe and from which financial aid administrators, both individually and as members of their own professional associations, have developed standards for themselves.[24]

Each of the more than 1,350 postsecondary institutions, secondary schools, and agencies that are members of the College Scholarship Service Assembly have agreed, through their chief executive officer, to support the statement. By its adoption, the member institutions of the CSS Assembly acknowledge that equality of educational opportunity can be realized only with fully funded and properly administered need-based programs of student financial assistance, and have affirmed their intent to work toward achieving these goals.

Principles of Student Financial Aid Administration

1. The purpose of any financial aid program — institutional, governmental, or private — should be to provide monetary assistance to students who can benefit from further education but who cannot do so without such assistance. The primary purpose of a collegiate financial aid program should be to provide financial assistance to accepted students who, without such aid, would be unable to attend that college.

2. Each college has an obligation to assist in realizing the national goal of equality of educational opportunity. The college, therefore, should work with schools, community groups, and other educational institutions in support of this goal.

3. The college should publish budgets that state total student expenses realistically including, where applicable, maintenance at home, commuting expenses, personal expenses, and necessary travel.

4. Parents are expected to contribute according to their means, taking into account their income, assets, number of dependents, and other relevant information. Students themselves are expected to contribute from their own assets and earnings, including appropriate borrowing against future earnings.

5. Financial aid should be offered only after determination that the resources of the family are insufficient to meet the student's educational expenses. The amount of aid offered should not exceed the amount needed to meet the difference between the student's total educational expenses and the family's resources.

6. The amount and type of self-help expected from students should be related to the circumstances of the individual. In the assignment of funds to those students designated to receive financial aid, the largest amounts of total grant assistance should go to students with the least ability to pay.

7. The college should review its financial assistance awards annually and adjust them, if necessary, to reflect changes in

the financial needs of students and the expenses of attending the institution. The college has an obligation to inform students and parents of the financial aid renewal policies for enrolled students at the time of the initial offer of financial assistance.

8. Because the amount of financial assistance awarded reflects the economic circumstances of students and their families, the college should refrain from any public announcement of the amount of aid offered, and encourage students, their secondary schools, and others to respect the confidentiality of this information.

9. All documents, correspondence, and conversations between and among aid applicants, their families, and financial aid officers are confidential and entitled to the protection ordinarily arising from a counseling relationship.

10. Concern for the student should be paramount. Financial aid should be administered in such a manner that other interests, important though they may be, are subordinate to the needs of students.

This statement of principles provides a broad, general, philosophical basis upon which institutions can focus the administration of their financial aid programs. It does not pretend to provide for every contingency that the aid administrator must face. Neither is it necessarily specific enough for every institution. With that in mind, the members of the College Scholarship Service Assembly endorsed, in 1973, a set of practices for the administration of financial aid programs to provide more guidance to institutions and to further help assure the equitable treatment of student aid applicants. The preamble of the statement indicates that "The increase in the number of students requiring financial aid in order to pursue postsecondary educational objectives and the increase in the number and variety of institutions awarding limited student aid funds require standards and guidelines for the responsible administration of student aid programs and the equitable distribution of funds. This statement of practices is intended to be used in conjunction with the Principles of Student Financial Aid Administration as a guide to institutions in the administration and coordination of their financial aid programs."

Practices of Student Financial Aid Administration

Motivation and information — Actively encourage students to utilize available financial aid services by

1. Coordinating efforts with those of federal, state, community, and other agencies as well as those of secondary schools to encourage all students who want to continue education beyond secondary school to consider postsecondary education regardless of their financial circumstances.

2. Providing complete and current written information to students and parents about financial aid policies, full costs of attendance, application procedures, eligibility criteria, and available student financial aid.

Counseling — Make explicit the need for student financial planning by

3. Cooperating with secondary schools and agencies in providing adequate guidance and counseling in financial planning.

4. Providing and maintaining financial counseling programs for all students who seek assistance.

Organization and administration — Establish administrative procedures that are responsive to the needs of students as well as the needs of institutions by

5. Conducting surveys to assist in the development of realistic student budgets.

6. Utilizing a recognized standard need analysis system consistently to determine the ability of students and their families to pay for educational costs.

7. Considering the student's individual circumstances when offering self-help aid and in determining the self-help expectation.

8. Using all forms of aid — grant, loan, employment — and considering other resources available to the student in order

to provide the most equitable apportionment of limited funds to eligible students.

9. Meeting the full need of students to the extent possible within the institution's capabilities.

10. Providing award notifications that clearly indicate the type, amount, and conditions of the award including the expected amount of family contribution and other anticipated resources.

11. Providing students who are not offered financial aid with the specific reason(s) for the denial of aid and, to the extent possible, assisting them in finding alternative sources of aid.

12. Making awards to students who apply for renewal of aid by reviewing the student's financial circumstances and establishing the amount of aid needed with full consideration of the student's current need.

13. Advising secondary schools and state and other granting agencies that it is inappropriate to announce individual or aggregate aid awards received by student applicants on the basis of need.

14. Releasing parents' or student's financial aid records and information only with the written consent of the parents or the student except in accordance with due process of law.

15. Considering the inclusion of students, faculty members, and administrators on institutional committees that are responsible for establishing financial aid policies.

16. Coordinating the administration of financial aid through a central office to ensure consistency in making awards to students and the most efficient use of available funds.

17. Notifying students of financial aid decisions as early as possible in order to serve the students' best interests, and when possible coordinating these notifications with those of admissions decisions.

18. Sharing information with other institutions and agencies about mutual aid candidates to ensure comparable financial aid awards, thereby permitting a student freedom in choosing an institution.

Research and professional development — Continue to contribute to the evaluation and progress of the profession of student financial aid administration by

19. Developing and conducting research programs that will contribute to the solution of problems and advancement of knowledge in the field of financial aid.

20. Conducting periodic reviews of the institution's total financial aid process in order to serve students and the institution better.

21. Encouraging the continued professional development of financial aid administrators by providing opportunities to join and participate in professional aid administrators' associations and organizations dedicated to the advancement of sound principles and practices and the extension of knowledge in student financial aid administration.

These practices must, of course, be implemented with consideration to the requirements (or limitations) of appropriate legislative authority. Privacy legislation at the state and federal level may limit institutions' ability to share information; consumerism legislation (discussed in more detail in the section on common problems) may mandate that particular kinds of information be made available to current and prospective students.

These principles and practices must also be implemented in the context of a particular postsecondary institution, its location, its programs and curriculums, its clientele of students, and especially its purposes. One of the most important characteristics of the model college financial aid office is that it must serve the purposes of the institution as well as meeting the needs of the students. Different kinds of financial aid and different methods of administering financial aid have different present-time and future-time implications for institutions. Awareness of those differences and their effects on institutional purposes is one of the hallmarks of good aid administration.

For example, if the purpose of a particular institution is to provide a highly concentrated education in science and technology — a program that requires long hours of class, laboratory, and study time — a policy of including in every student aid package an expectation of self-help predicated on term-time employment may act contrary to the achievement of the purposes of the institution. Another institution with the purpose of serving as a focus for an urban community by providing educational experiences to train future community leaders might suggest a vigorous and extensive off-campus work-study program that would serve as a major component of most students' aid packages.

Administrative Organization
of the Financial Aid Office

Administrative Structure

Before 1958, the administration of student financial aid at many institutions required little time each year. The responsibility may have been discharged by a single individual, perhaps a dean, or by an occasionally assembled "staff" that constituted a temporary "ad hoc" committee to conduct the program in an intuitive and benevolent manner. Frequently, there was no higher authority who supervised the activity and no one, other than the fiscal officer, who required an accounting. Seldom, if ever, was there even a formal rationale within which to function.

As aid resources have increased in importance both to the institutions and to the students, and as the number of students applying for aid has increased, the organizational structure of student financial aid offices has been reconsidered and revised by almost every institution. Specific individuals are now assigned responsibility for the various student financial aid procedures, and these individuals occupy specified positions in the administrative organization of the institution.

It is interesting to note that in spite of the increase in the importance of the financial aid function, slightly fewer directors of financial aid responding to the 1978 NASFAA survey said that they devoted all of their time to aid administration than had been true in a survey conducted in 1970 by Warren Willingham.

In the 1970 survey, 60 percent of the responding institutions had a full-time director.[25] In the 1978 NASFAA survey only 56.7 percent of the responding directors said that they devoted all their employment time to financial aid work (although more than 93 percent of them said that they were full-time employees of their institution). Of the nonaid time, just under 20 percent of it was reportedly spent on admissions work, about 15 percent in the business office, just over 12 percent in the dean of students office, but only 8 percent in teaching and 4 percent in counseling.[26]

In 1966 Ayers, Tripp, and Russell reported that in about half of all institutions the individual responsible for the administration of financial aid reported directly to the president.[27] This report was generally in agreement with that of Nash and Lazarsfeld, who found that 46 percent of the aid administrators reported to the college president.[28] The more recent NASFAA survey has found major changes in this administrative alignment. Among the 1978 NASFAA respondents only 13 percent of directors said that they reported directly to the president or chief administrative officer of their institution. Proprietary institutions did have more than half (57.4 percent) of their directors reporting to the chief administrative officer, but at independent private institutions only 13 percent indicated this reporting relationship. At the public institutions only 5 percent said that they reported directly to their president.[29]

As Table 2 indicates for all institutions responding to the NASFAA survey, the most common chain of command was from the director of student aid to the institution's chief student personnel officer. There were, however, significant differences in these relationships among the different kinds of institutions. While more than two thirds of the public institutions' directors of aid reported to the student personnel administrator, only slightly more than one quarter of the independent private institutions had this reporting relationship. Independent private institutions were significantly more likely to lodge their financial aid activities under the supervision of the chief business officer or director of admissions than was true at the public institutions. Very few institutions, regardless of type, reported that their financial aid activities were supervised by the chief *academic* officer.[30]

The current administrative alignments of financial aid directors in postsecondary institutions developed during a period that one administrator has characterized as having a "surplus of students and a shortage of dollars." The future may

*Table 2. The Aid Administrator's Immediate
Superior by Type of Institution*

	Public	Private	Proprietary	All
President or chief administrative officer .	5.3%	13.0%	57.4%	13.4%
Chief business officer.	4.6	19.3	3.2	11.9
Chief academic officer	2.1	6.4	1.1	4.2
Chief student personnel officer or dean of students	67.4	27.8	8.6	42.7
Director of admissions	2.1	11.1	1.1	6.6
Manager or administrator	.6	1.0	9.5	1.6
Other	17.9	21.4	19.1	19.7

alter that relationship—surely there will be a shortage of students for the next decade. It will be interesting to see if the percentage of institutions aligning financial aid with the admissions office changes as more emphasis is placed on the role of
aid in attracting students from a more limited pool of prospects.

Role of the Advisory Committee on Financial Aid

A survey conducted by the College Scholarship Service's Panel
on Student Financial Need Analysis in 1969–70 showed that in
the 84 institutions responding, the financial aid administrator
was predominantly responsible for the decisions made about
the applications of individual students, while policy decisions
that guide the making of individual awards were predominantly
made by committees (see Table 3).[31] The more recent NASFAA
survey did not inquire into the relative roles of the administrator or the committee in the decision-making process, but a
memorandum from the NASFAA Committee on Program Review
begins with a recommendation "that a Financial Aid Committee
be an integral part of the operation at institutions which participate in Federal Student Financial Aid Programs. . . ."[32]

The NASFAA recommendation continues: "Generally, the
rationale for the existence of a Financial Aid Committee would
be to keep in focus the perspective of the total institution—i.e.

Table 3. Institutional Decision-Making on Financial Aid Policy and Individual Applications for Aid

Decision-maker	Individual decisions			Policy decisions		
	Public	Private	Total	Public	Private	Total
Aid officer	32	34	66	11	9	20
Admissions officer	—	3	3		2	2
Faculty committee	—	1	1	1	3	4
Faculty administrative committee	6	4	10	10	19	29
Faculty administrative student committee	3	1	4	17	8	25
Other officer.	—	—	—	2	2	4
Total	41	43	84	41	43	84

students, faculty, administration and primary providers of funding—in the development and periodic review of institutional financial aid policies." In addition, the advisory committee should be aware of and understand the national trends in student financial aid, and the ways in which these trends would and should affect the institution. The committee periodically should review the general operations of the aid office to insure that policy is reflected in procedures. To avoid becoming isolated from the students, the committee should serve as an appeal board for students who believe their requests for aid were not treated appropriately.

The advisory committee provides a means by which representation may be obtained from the several divisions of the institution, and it provides a vehicle to bring the perspectives of the various parts of the academic community to bear on the formulation and supervision of the institution's policy on student financial aid.

The normal procedures for establishing and staffing committees, and for selecting or appointing committee chairpersons, should be followed in initiating and in continuing the advisory committee on financial aid. All parts of the institution should be involved in the development of a policy on financial aid in order that the policy be truly representative of the institution.

The committee should have as members representatives of the fiscal, student personnel services, registrars, and admissions staffs, as well as of the teaching faculty. Including students as members of the committee is recognized as extremely important by most institutions and most financial aid officers. The director of financial aid should serve as secretary to the committee. The advisory committee should be the body that brings recommendations for action to the attention of the appropriate officials.

Staffing

Obtaining enough staff to operate in an efficient and effective manner has been, and continues to be, one of the foremost problems facing financial aid administrators. Progress made in other areas — more student aid, more programs to serve broader constituencies, more needy students encouraged to apply, greater sophistication in the process and processing of aid applications — all seem to increase the stress on the office staff. In the 1968 Bureau of Applied Social Research study, half of the respondents contended that they were without an adequate number of clerical personnel to meet their duties in student aid administration.[33] In a survey conducted by the College Board in 1977–78 about one third of the respondents said that the size of their professional staff was less than adequate, about half said that the support staff was not large enough to be considered adequate, and more than one third said that their student employee complement was not large enough to be adequate.[34] The caution of the National Association of College and University Business Officers, delivered in 1972, continues to be ignored: "schools cannot continue to overburden the person in charge of financial aid programs . . ." by failing to provide a staff adequate in both quality and quantity.[35]

It is difficult because of the variety of tasks that may be

assigned to a particular office and the number of different aid programs it may administer to postulate optimum numbers of professional and clerical staff for the operation of the financial aid office. There has been considerable discussion of the basis to use in determining the appropriate number of staff members. Most early staffing formulas were based on the number of students enrolled at the institution. Subsequently, formulas were developed on the basis of the number of financial aid recipients. It now appears that a more appropriate basis is the number of students who apply for financial assistance. It requires at least as much staff time (if not more) to process an application that must be denied, communicate that decision to the applicant, and assist in the identification of alternative sources of financing for him as it does to process an application that is ultimately approved. The data from the 1977 College Board study suggest that the following *minimum* staff complements would seem to be required for adequate administration:

1. Every financial aid office should have at least *one* full-time equivalent professional staff member and *one* full-time equivalent support staff member.

2. Institutions with between 500 and 1,000 aid applicants should have at least *two* full-time equivalent professional staff members and *two* full-time equivalent support staff members.

3. For *each additional* 1,000 financial aid applicants the institution should add at least *one* full-time equivalent professional staff member and at least *two* full-time equivalent support staff members.

4. Institutions should have at least *two* full-time equivalent student staff members for every 1,000 financial aid applicants.[36]

The last element of this recommendation is one which many aid administrators are unwilling to adopt — or at least they are unwilling to use students in any but clerical capacities — because of concern about the sensitivity of the data with which the office must deal. Those who maintain this concern and continue to express dismay about the size of their staff might consider the comment of Edward Sanders, one of the "deans" of student aid, when he observed of the admissions profession, "The argument that a college senior is incapable of dealing with confidential materials, whereas the day after he graduates he is competent to become an admissions officer suggests a confidence in the value of touching a sheepskin that I do not share."[37]

In very large institutions the use of standardized forms and the adaptation of routine procedures to utilize the capabilities of automatic data-processing machinery may reduce the need for increasing the number of clerical employees. If the financial aid office is assigned responsibilities for activities other than the actual administration of the student aid programs (such as collecting loans, accounting, bookkeeping, academic or vocational counseling, and veterans affairs), these proposed staff requirements must be increased to allow for the additional duties that would have to be undertaken.

Earlier staffing formula recommendations suggested the ways in which the positions should be assigned (director, assistant director, administrative assistant, etc.) within the office. Since that depends to a large degree on the organizational structure that the office assumes, or that which is imposed upon it by the organization of the institution, such recommendations no longer seem relevant. Some administrative organization alternatives that might be considered in larger offices would be:

1. *By function.* The staff might be divided between those in the front office responsible for day-to-day communication and interaction with students and the "back office" staff responsible for processing applications, calculating need, maintaining records, preparing reports, conducting research, etc.

2. *By type of student served.* Some part of the office staff might be responsible for all activity relating to new applicants; others to continuing or renewal candidates.

3. *By institutional division.* In a complex institution it is frequently appropriate to divide the work of the office along divisional lines — some staff assigned to work with students

from each individual college, some assigned to undergraduate students and others to graduate and professional students, or some similar division of labor appropriate to the organization of the institution.

The use of a common application providing consideration for all available student aid, the centralization of aid activities into a single office, and the nearly universal practice of "packaging" grant, loan, and work offers to try to meet the total need of a student seem to make it generally inappropriate to divide the labor of the office along program lines. The exception frequently is in the area of work assistance, where the post-award requirement of interviewing, referral, placement, and follow-up suggest to some administrators that there be a work-study coordinator specializing in such activities.

Some institutions have turned to outside firms and consultants to handle the operations of their financial aid activities. In some cases the services provided are comprehensive, including completion of the institution's application for federal funds, providing applications for students to complete, processing complete applications and determining eligibility for assistance, making awards, monitoring institutional disbursements of funds to students, handling loan collections, and completing the required federal reports. In other cases the services are specific to a particular element of the aid operation, such as loan billing and collection.

Some of these outside firms are part of larger organizations (such as banks or commercial collection agencies) with other activities accounting for a major part of their business. In other cases they are individuals with prior experience in financial aid, some currently affiliated with another institution but others devoting their entire time to the administration of aid for smaller institutions. The charges that these organizations and individuals levy for their services typically include a retainer plus so much per student application processed or per account handled. In some instances the charges reflect a percentage of the amount of federal or other funds that the firm can produce for the use of students at the educational institution.

There currently are no standards or criteria against which an institution can evaluate the desirability or effectiveness of this method of administration. In the case of organizations with other activities or with an established history in aid management the experience of previous (and continuing) clients can provide some guidance to an institution. In other cases a "trial period" may be appropriate before entering into a long-term arrangement with an outside firm or individual consultant.

The determination of adequate levels of compensation for financial aid office personnel must be based, among other considerations, on an evaluation of the responsibilities assigned to the office, the professional preparation of the candidates, the experience required for the position, and the general levels of local salary scales. The 1978 NASFAA study reported data on the salary of the directors of student aid at public, independent private, and proprietary institutions (see Table 4).[38]

Table 4. Annual Salaries of College Financial Aid Officers, 1978

Salary	Public	Private	Proprietary
Under $9,000	1.0%	5.2%	11.7%
$9,000 to $10,999	2.3	12.8	20.2
$11,000 to $12,999	2.5	18.2	22.3
$13,000 to $14,999	10.3	19.4	16.0
$15,000 to $16,999	16.5	14.9	11.7
$17,000 to $18,999	16.9	10.2	5.3
$19,000 to $20,999	16.7	9.2	1.1
$21,000 to $23,999	18.0	5.7	2.1
$24,000 to $26,999	8.8	2.6	4.3
$27,000 or above	6.9	1.9	5.3
Median	$19,050	$14,430	$12,620

That the salaries paid to directors of financial aid continue to be low relative to other institutional administrators is demonstrated by data provided by a survey conducted by the College and University Personnel Association (see Table 5).[39]

Most of the directors of financial aid responding to the 1978

Table 5. Median Salaries of College Administrators, 1978–79

	All	Public	Private
Chief executive officer*	$40,000	$41,500	$37,500
Chief academic officer.	32,000	35,000	28,000
Chief business officer	29,500	31,860	26,500
Director of admissions.	21,000	22,392	19,000
Director of counseling.	21,475	23,085	17,700
Director of placement	18,119	20,500	15,270
Director of financial aid	18,020	20,226	15,300
Director of bookstore	14,073	16,300	11,687

* Single institution, rather than segment, responsibilities.

NASFAA survey were themselves college graduates. Only 10 percent did not acknowledge that they held any college degree. More than half reported that they held advanced degrees, with 52 percent indicating the receipt of a masters degree and 5 percent reporting a doctorate.[40] The level of academic achievement in the NASFAA survey group was somewhat lower than that reported by Nash and Lazarsfeld a decade earlier. Seventeen percent of the directors in that study had completed the requirements for a doctorate and 66 percent had earned a masters degree.[41]

One organizational issue of major concern a decade ago — the need to implement a centralized office responsible for the administration of all kinds of financial assistance — no longer seems a problem. In the NASFAA survey, more than 95 percent of the directors said that their office would be considered the central office for financial aid administration on their campus.[42] While some graduate and professional divisions of complex institutions continue to maintain separate financial aid offices to serve their particular student clientele, the centralization of undergraduate financial aid into a single office at each institution seems virtually complete.

Functions of the Financial Aid Office

The actual functions to be performed by the personnel of the financial aid office will vary according to the specific responsibilities assigned to it and the programs under its jurisdiction. There is, however, a central core of activities that must be carried out to achieve successful administration of the obligations basic to any aid office. The following outline presents an overview of the most common of these activities.

I. Counseling about typical student expenses, financial aid opportunities, problems associated with borrowing
   A. Conduct regularly scheduled meetings to provide needed information to specific groups
      1. Before admission to college
         a. Potential students, both first-time freshmen and transfer students who request information
         b. Applicants for financial aid
         c. Parents' groups
      2. During the students' college years
         a. Aid applicants
         b. Aid recipients
         c. Students failing to make normal progress or planning to transfer or withdraw
      3. Before graduation
         a. Aid recipients
         b. Potential applicants to graduate and professional schools who request information
      4. Local scholarship donor groups
   B. Confer with individual students, on the initiative either of the student or of the financial aid administrator
      1. Student expense budgeting
      2. Personal and family situations that might be related to financial needs and opportunities or changes in family circumstances
      3. Student rights and responsibilities

  4. Money management
II. General administration
 A. Supervise office functions
  1. Develop and review financial aid applications and other forms used in the administration of aid programs
  2. Develop and review student consumerism materials
  3. Establish, and document in a written manual, office routines and procedures
  4. Assign duties to office personnel and document in written job descriptions
  5. Provide routine supervision to personnel
  6. Organize and implement an in-service training and development program for office personnel
 B. Review state and federal legislative changes to assure institutional conformity with provisions
  1. Issue new directives to office personnel
  2. Provide informational memoranda to others at the institution and in the community concerned with matters relating to student aid
  3. Update office forms, procedures, policies, and manuals
 C. Review applications for financial aid
  1. Evaluate financial status of the applicants in connection with aid programs that require demonstration of financial need
  2. Evaluate supporting records of the applicants, e.g., personal, academic, etc.
  3. Determine eligibility of the applicants for consideration for the several types of programs within the three major forms of aid
 D. Allocate aid resources
  1. Select applicants to whom aid will be awarded
  2. Determine the amount of aid to be awarded and how the different kinds of aid will be packaged to meet student needs

3. Notify recipients, in writing, of the way in which their need was determined, the amounts and forms in which aid is being offered to them, and any conditions of the aid offered
4. Notify students who can not be aided of the reasons why their applications could not be approved, alternative sources that may be available to them, and procedures that they may follow if their circumstances change
5. Inform students who accept offered assistance regarding the procedures they must follow to secure disbursements or to have awards properly credited to their accounts at registration, how to continue to remain eligible, and how to request renewal funds
6. Assure that proper required documentation is included in every student's file
7. Review any student appeals according to institutional policy and procedures established by the advisory committee

E. Authorize disbursement of funds
1. Report to the appropriate fiscal authority on the campus the amount and form of each award made and the dates and amounts of individual disbursements to students
2. Describe any contingencies on the release of funds
3. Cancel unclaimed awards and reallocate funds to other students

F. Review and plan
1. Evaluate the functions and activities of the aid office
2. Prepare planning memorandums for aid office activities in future years
3. Prepare proposed budgets of student aid funds
4. Prepare budget requests for the staff and the operation of the aid office
5. Hold regular staff meetings to collect information

and advice about how operations could be improved
6. Prepare recommendations for changes in the institution's policies for student financial aid
7. Attend and participate in meetings concerned with the development of institutional policies on financial aid

III. Motivation of students (in cooperation with the admissions office, the offices of special programs, etc.)
  A. Visit secondary schools and community colleges
    1. Participate in meetings and discussions on the general topic of attending college
    2. Assist in programs and activities designed to stimulate interest in attending a particular college
  B. Conduct workshops and other informational activities on financial aid
    1. Faculty for various groups, administrators, and students within postsecondary institutions
    2. Secondary school and community college administrators and faculty
    3. Secondary school and community college students and their parents
    4. Community agencies, educational information centers, and other nonschool sources concerned with guidance and counseling prospective students
    5. Special agencies serving target populations such as racial or ethnic minorities, senior citizens, or women
    6. Civic, patriotic, and fraternal organizations

IV. Development of aid resources
  A. Calculate aggregate financial need
    1. Of currently enrolled students
    2. Of potential students who might be enrolled under different policies or procedures
  B. Describe the status and needs of particular groups of students who might be of interest to potential donors and sponsors of funds
    1. Arrange individual appointments and meetings with

persons who might provide funds or employment opportunities

    2. Participate in the programs of local organizations who might sponsor student aid funds

  C. Develop or support recommendations for legislative changes or new government student aid programs

  D. Continue to cooperate and to consult with representatives of existing sources of funds

V. Research and evaluation

  A. Initiate and continue evaluations of the aid program of the institution

  B. Conduct and encourage studies on the impact of the aid program on the students and the institution

  C. Summarize applications

    1. At the close of each awarding period, or at least annually, review applications for financial aid

    2. Gather data on such characteristics of the applicant group as sex, ethnic background, family size, income, student expense budgets, and self-help provided from noninstitutional sources

  D. Review patterns of aid offer acceptance, rejection, and modification to refine packaging procedures and allowable over-commitment to assure full utilization of funds

  E. Initiate self-audits of the aid operation and participate in external audits and program reviews

  F. Prepare necessary reports

    1. Annual report to the institution

    2. Reports to agencies of the state and federal governments both to recapitulate activities and to initiate requests for additional funds

    3. Annual report to the donors or sponsors of funds

Pervading all these operational activities is the general need for the financial aid office to be active in the process of providing information to prospective students. A variety of studies, summarized in Table 6, have demonstrated the consistent im-

Table 6. Highlights of Findings about Prospective Student Information Needs*

css *Student Committee (Interviews about financial aid problems)*	css *and the College Board (Survey of cost and aid information needs)*
■ Lack of information about financial aid was the single most frequently expressed problem	■ 4 of 10 students said they would have planned to attend a different institution were cost not a factor
■ Lack of integration of financial aid information with admissions, counseling, and employment processes	■ Strong relationship between information needs and income-level and ethnicity
■ Lack of information on specific filing deadlines	■ Students want both total cost and other general information as well as detailed aid information
■ Special problems for transfer students	■ Information rated as highly important included
	— how and when costs must be paid
	— total cost of entire degree program
	— probability of changes in cost year to year
	— detailed descriptions of kinds of aid available
	— what kinds of aid go to people like them
	— specific information on available jobs
	— how to apply and deadlines
	— loan repayment procedures

portance of information about costs and aid in the decisions of people considering postsecondary education.[43] The federal government, as part of the Education Amendments of 1976, mandated a core of consumer-related information that the

NCHEMS, *Guidebook* *(Survey of wide variety of information needed about colleges, multiple states)*	*Oregon data* *(Survey of wide variety of information needed about colleges, Oregon only)*
■ Prospective students remain unsure about the appropriate questions to ask when selecting a college	■ Top 10 areas of importance were
■ Areas of information rated high in importance across all groups included	— courses required for major and graduation
— admission/dropout/transfer information	— future demand in certain job/skill areas
— financial aid information (typical amounts of aid given to students by level and at different income levels)	— qualifications for job entry
— housing and student services information	— difficulty entering a specific program
— out-of-class activity opportunities	— admission application and test deadlines
— information about instruction and instructors (extensive needs)	— transferability of credits
— information about college major	— time it takes to graduate
— college impact on last year's graduates (extensive needs)	— total cost to complete a program
■ Special information needs identified for minority, transfer, adult, and graduate students	— is a degree needed for an area of interest?
	— how many graduates of a particular program get the jobs they apply for?
	■ Relatively high ratings given to items about costs, programs, and career information
	■ Relatively low availability of information given to items related to results of attendance, careers, support services, social life, and financial support

* Master Plan Task Force on Student Assistance Information, *Prospective Students' Need for Information about Financial Aid and Costs: A Review of the Literature.* Trenton, N.J.: State of New Jersey Department of Higher Education, 1978, p. 7.

financial aid office must provide (discussed in the section on some common problems). This federally mandated information, however, must be supplemented with an active campaign by the institution to provide more extensive and more specific information to meet the needs of different groups of prospective students.

Another activity of the aid office that should characterize all its behavior is that of student advocacy in respect to financial matters. In addition to providing the means with which students can pay institutional and other charges, the aid office should play an active role in the development, review, and modification of policies and procedures concerning charges and the method of their payment. An obvious example is in the considerations of changes in the level of tuition and fees. While those decisions must be made on the basis of general institutional needs and budgets, the aid office should represent the specific interests of students by informing senior administration of the impact that a tuition and fee increase will have on students, the amount that can be off-set through increases in financial aid available from noninstitutional sources, and the amount of the increase that should be "returned" to students through institutionally provided aid in order to at least maintain "parity." Other areas in which the aid office should adopt an advocacy role are those relating to the schedules for payment of required charges, pay rates for student employees, and the provision of such services as medical or child care.

The list of functions of the aid office presented here does not include the actual disbursement of funds to students or the collection of loans. These are properly the functions of other offices of the institution (for legal as well as technical reasons). However, because activities in these two areas vitally concern the success of the aid office in achieving its objectives of supporting students and fostering the purposes of the institution, the aid administrator must remain cognizant of the status of these activities and actively participate in the formulation of policies and procedures under which they are carried out.

Relations within the Institution

Since student financial aid serves to support and to extend both the general purposes and the particular programs of the institution of higher learning, the director of student aid and his staff necessarily must communicate frequently with the faculty and with the administrative staffs of other activities and programs on the campus. Although student financial aid activities impinge on every area of activity within the institution, associations with some areas are more frequent and the communications more critical than with others.

Faculty and Academic Activities

Because the development and transmission of knowledge and skills are among the major goals of every postsecondary institution, the student financial aid program must function in support of the institution's academic and instructional goals and programs. The basic principles described earlier as guiding the operations of the student aid program do not preclude involvement in activities designed to recognize academic accomplishment, to enroll and retain qualified students, and to assist in the achievement of the goals set for academic counseling and student discipline. Indeed, those principles suggest the educational role of the aid administrator and provide the parameters within which these academic activities may be conducted.

The faculty can and should be a source of strong support for the student aid activities. Through membership on the financial aid advisory committee, the faculty is able to participate in establishing policies, practices, and procedures for the operation of the student aid program. As members of the advisory committee, the faculty can serve as an appeal board for students to assure that the daily administrative functions are being carried on in accord with the institutional principles, policies, and procedures. The faculty may also be able to serve in the area of developing sources of grant and loan funds through their off-campus association with potential donors of aid resources. In addition, the faculty is one of the largest and most educationally worthwhile sources of employment for students.

While the role of faculty as employer can provide a valuable resource to the financial aid administrator, this role can also produce problems. Many institutions today are faced with continuing and deepening cuts in funds available for both part-time and regular employment. When budgetary limitations reduce the amount of regular budgeted monies available for assistance, the faculty will naturally turn to the part-time and college work-study employment programs to find employees needed to perform educationally related jobs. The aid administrator may encounter difficulties in maintaining the federally mandated position that the College Work-Study Program is primarily a source of financial aid and that any benefit that accrues to the institution or particular segments of the institution must be secondary.

Admissions Office

Perhaps one of the most significant administrative relationships for the aid office is that with the admissions office. Even though the two functions are most typically separated, "it is still evident that student aid policies can modify the most carefully considered admissions program. . . ."[43] Careful coordination of policy and activities is important if the institutional mission is to be successfully discharged. This kind of coordination will become even more important as the pools of potential students from the traditional college-going population decline and institutions seek to reach new and different clienteles. The institution's ability to do this will depend on a close and constant working relationship between the personnel of the admissions office and those of the financial aid office.

To a certain extent, the admissions office is the source of

44

candidates for the financial aid program. Both offices are concerned with many of the same students before registration. Because the admissions office typically is responsible for establishing the institution's first data file about new students, information that is collected and evaluated in the admissions process can provide the aid office with necessary data (prior education and achievement, future plans, etc.). Too, the admissions office is in the position of having extensive, if not almost continuous, communications with secondary school personnel, applicants, and their families. Thus information about the aid program and its requirements can frequently be distributed through the admissions office in ways and at times particularly relevant to the postsecondary decision-making process.

The aid office can be supportive of the admissions office's recruiting efforts by supplying vital information on the characteristics of aid candidates and recipients who actually enroll or who fail to attend. As increasing numbers of institutions face enrollment difficulties, the financial aid office will become an even more important source of data that the admissions staff can utilize in predicting actual enrollments and in locating prospective students. Because of the interdependency of these responsibilities and the compelling need to communicate adequately with prospective students and their families, the staff of each office is deeply concerned with the work of the other office.

Another area of administrative interrelationships deals with the matter of the admissions application fee. Most institutions with such fees have arrangements to waive them for low-income students. The financial aids office can assist the admissions office in determining when such waivers may be appropriate. In addition, student applications for fee waivers can be cross-checked with aid applications to assure that those who may need more assistance than a fee waiver are aware that the institution may be able to provide it.

Special Program Offices

Most institutions have established special programs to deal with the particular needs of different groups of students. Institutions frequently have formal programs to identify, motivate, and admit students from low-income families and from racial and ethnic minority groups. More recently similar programs have developed to serve the special needs of other groups such as displaced homemakers, older students, the handicapped, and former convicts. Program content differs from institution to institution, but typically the provision of data about costs and available aid, assistance in completion of aid applications, and advocacy in securing assistance are an important part of the programs.

Close relationships between the aid office and the staffs of these kinds of special programs are particularly important. One of the characteristics of most of the students recruited through these programs is that their financial circumstances, for one reason or another, are bad. They may come from low-income families or may be suddenly shifted out of situations where others cared for their needs. Frequently they will have less flexibility in modifying existing housing, employment, or other aspects of their situation than is true of the typical aid applicant. In many cases their expenses may be significantly higher than usual. They may also come from circumstances requiring more concern for confidentiality than is normally the case, as with ex-felons or individuals in drug-rehabilitation programs.

The staffs of these special program offices typically will be in day-to-day communication with individuals in the community who are themselves potential students or who are in a position to identify potential students. It is vitally important, therefore, that the special program personnel have complete and current information about available student aid programs and policies. Specially prepared and scheduled training workshops provided by the aid office will help to maintain this information level. The aid office might also want to include representatives of special program offices in its regular staff meetings. This can provide a two-way communication of problems and opportunities. Participation of the special program personnel in the formulation of policy recommendations can help preclude the implementation of policies detrimental to their efforts to recruit particular groups of students.

Frequently, the staffs of the special program offices are more involved in the actual process of completing aid application materials than is true of the admissions office staff. It may be appropriate to provide individuals who have this responsibility with more training in the actual application-processing procedures than would be true for other offices' staffs. The special program staffs also may be more informed about and more sensitive to the special and often unique needs of their service populations. This may suggest more involvement on their part in the actual aid decision-making process than would be true for counselors in offices not as directly informed about or concerned with their students' financial circumstances and needs. The staff of a special program office may be able to provide valuable advice to the aid office about the effectiveness of its communications, forms, and other written materials in reaching populations for whom written English may not be the most effective form of communication. Translating financial aid materials into another language may be essential to reaching some potential populations; special program personnel can identify those for which this may be appropriate and in many cases can actually provide the needed translations.

Business and Accounting Office

The business and accounting office and the aid office constitute another area of mutual administrative dependency. Because it deals with money, the aid office is perceived by many as a business function. There is a strong need for a harmonious relationship in the reporting and recording of both incoming money to be added to student aid funds and of the commitments against and actual disbursements from those accounts made by the business office to students upon approval of the aid office. The reporting and the research activities of the student aid office necessarily concern both students and money; therefore, coordination between the business office and the aid office is a virtual necessity if reports are to be prepared accurately and on schedule.

The business office may be the first point at which a student's financial problems become known. In connection with student loan accounts the need for coordination between the financial aid and business offices becomes acute. As the Oregon Educational Coordinating Commission has noted, "The recirculation of NDSL program dollars to other students after repayment means that the amount of the federal allocations remains at the disposal of the individual institutions indefinitely. Because of this, the institutions are less dependent upon new allocations for programs."[44] Unless the business office has the data necessary to assure prompt repayment of loans, and has that data at times and in ways appropriate to the exercise of "due diligence," the institution's total financial aid program may be unduly hampered.

The relationship between the financial aid and business offices is also of longer duration than is true in other cases. The Oregon report continues, "this same characteristic means that the administrative burden which the [NDSL] program places upon participating institutions is a cumulative process which grows larger and more complex with every passing year of program operation. . . . Federal grant and work programs put money at the disposal of the institutions for one fiscal year at a time, and the workload for the institutions is proportional to the volume of annual disbursements. In the NDSL program, the total workload is proportional to the cumulative amount of disbursements which have been made since the beginning of the program." This cumulative and long-term relationship requires that the business officer and the aid director join forces to exert their combined skill and knowledge in the collection of student loans.

The administration of a work-study program also requires close cooperation between the business office and the aid office. Student employment is neither as regular nor as predictable as that of "regular" employees, and changes in hours, rates of pay, and places of employment can reasonably be expected to occur with frequency. Close coordination and cooperation between the aid office and the "paymaster" is important if students are to be assured a regular source of income from employment.

Registration and Records Offices

Substantially all financial aid programs require that recipients maintain normal progress toward degrees or certificates and exhibit satisfactory standards of academic achievement. To be able to ascertain that this condition is being met and to intervene when it is not, the financial aid office must have access to data from the office of the registrar or the central records of the institution. This requires the development and maintenance of close working relationships between these offices and the financial aid staff.

The need to prepare and return reports in connection with major programs of student assistance sponsored by the federal government has reinforced the necessity, particularly in large institutions, of cooperation among the aid director and the directors of the various records and registration operations. For institutions that must also submit reports to statewide governing or coordinating boards, the need for such cooperation is further heightened.

Data Processing Center

One of the relationships most rapidly developing in importance for the aid office is that with the data processing center. More and more offices have been able to maintain their level of service and program administration only through the use of automatic data processing systems. Some elements involved in the development and implementation of such systems are described in the section on some common problems, but one characteristic of all financial aid data processing systems is that they require very close cooperation between the staff of the aid office and the staff of the data processing center. Some institutions have attempted to foster this close relationship by employing in the aid office individuals whose primary area of competence is in data processing. In other institutions, the director of aid or key members of the aid office staff have acquired at least passing familiarity with the details of data processing systems. Others have simply developed good relationships of mutual trust and respect with personnel of the computer center. Regardless of the way in which it occurs, any institution with a good data processing system in support of its financial aid operation also has a good interpersonal relationship between the staffs of these two offices.

Even for institutions without formal financial aid data processing systems, this relationship is important. The reports required by federal and state agencies combine data from many institutional files. As these aid programs have continued to grow over the years, it has become increasingly difficult to maintain accurate and accessible records over long periods of time without access to some form of data processing support. This problem is particularly acute in very large institutions, where it is almost physically impossible to maintain the records necessary to report adequately on student aid activities without the assistance of electronic data processing equipment and personnel.

Dean of Students Office and Counseling, Testing, and Health Centers

In dealing with students and their problems, the financial aid administrator will frequently be in close communication with the various academic, vocational, and psychological counseling services, and with the university health services. Although the institution may have established various counseling offices and agencies to deal with specific kinds of problems, students will not always seek out the most appropriate agency or person directly. They may not perceive the real basis of their difficulties, or they may simply go to individuals with whom they have had previous communication and with whom they feel comfortable.

The financial aid administrator must be aware of the type and complexity of problems that are beyond the personal and professional qualifications of the aid office staff. When students come to the aid office with such problems, the staff must be able to make quick and appropriate referrals to other, more specialized, counseling services and to elicit agreements from the students for such referrals.

The aid office will frequently find that financial difficulties have caused, or have been caused by, physical or emotional problems. In these instances, the aid office staff must have the ability and inclination to refer students to the appropriate institutional or community facilities. The aid office must also be prepared to receive referrals from the staff of counseling and health facilities when they discover difficulties that have financial roots or ramifications.

Counselors of students who, while receiving financial aid encounter academic, disciplinary, or other behavioral problems, will be able to function with more confidence when they realize that financial aid can be adjusted to meet individual circumstances. The director of financial aid can be of marked assistance to counselors by rearranging, when necessary, the financial aid award package to permit a change in an academic schedule, an alteration in the hours of employment, or an adjustment in the amount of a loan.

Development and Alumni Offices

At some institutions, alumni and other private benefactors continue to be an important source of funds for student aid programs. An institution that is able to encourage continued financial support for student aid from alumni and from other donors is able to develop and to maintain a flexible and responsive aid program to meet particular situations. A financial aid program based exclusively on the use of governmental funds cannot be as flexible and responsive to student needs as it should be.

Although each institution probably can cite examples of occasions when special funds were needed to meet particular circumstances, a general use of such private aid funds would be a special short-term "emergency" loan program. It is difficult for a student to provide sufficient planning to meet all his financial needs for the academic year—a check may be delayed, a payroll card may be misplaced, a car may break down, eyeglasses may need to be repaired, or an unexpected trip home may be required. Limited loan programs usually do not require detailed financial information in the determination of eligibility; normally they are predicated upon the acceptance of a student's statement that an immediate need exists. Such loans are usually limited to small amounts and the repayment period typically is quite short. These kinds of programs do not encourage fiscal irresponsibility nor do they thwart the discipline of self-denial; they do recognize that plans may go awry and that there may be a short-term need that cannot be met from any other source.

While the limited emergency loan fund has appeal to alumni and other donors, few institutions will wish to restrict their activities to raising student aid money only for such programs. The aid director has a responsibility to work with the development officer and the alumni secretary in their efforts to develop and maintain sources of financial support for all types of student aid.

Relations with Off-Campus Agencies and Individuals

Members of the higher education establishment have been characterized as "the gatekeepers of the upper-middle class."[45] The financial aid administrator is frequently viewed by the community at large as one of the most important and effective gatekeepers of them all. In addition to the necessary on-campus relationships, the effective operation of the financial aid office requires good communications and close working relationships with a number of individuals and agencies outside the postsecondary institution. Most important among these are the schools from which students come, talent search agencies in the community, representatives of the sources of aid funds, agencies employing students, and colleagues in other aid offices on other campuses.

Secondary Schools and Community Colleges

Until recent years the role of the student financial aid administrator as a recruiter was essentially a passive one. The aid office received and evaluated requests for aid initiated by students and their parents. Now student aid administrators have taken on a more active role in the work of identifying, motivating, and encouraging students.

Usually information about financial aid that is made available to secondary school students and potential college transfer applicants is disseminated by the admissions offices, or in the case of special target populations, through the special program offices mentioned in the previous chapter. The obligations of institutions to seek out students from economically deprived areas who *must* have financial assistance if they are to attend makes it essential for aid office personnel to be closely involved in whatever communications the college has with secondary schools. In some instances it may be appropriate for the aid office staff to work with secondary school personnel without the coincident action of the admissions staff. Wherever possible, however, the aid office staff should take advantage of established channels of communication to avoid undue burdens on secondary school staffs.

Most secondary schools have programs that involve general college-bound counseling rather than programs centering on specific colleges; in these programs increasingly heavy emphasis is placed on the types and availability of financial aid resources. Because of frequent changes in regulations and procedures regarding student aid programs sponsored by federal and state governments, it is difficult for members of the admissions staff and school counselors to keep themselves sufficiently well informed to describe comprehensively the programs in specific terms to an audience that seeks information about financing an education beyond the high school. Assisting prospective college students and their parents by explaining ways of meeting educational expenses regardless of the institution to be selected is a service responsibility that can best be discharged by the aid director and his staff.

The growing importance of transfer programs in two-year community colleges has created another important area of activity for the aid director at a four-year college or university. In financial terms, a student who transfers from a community college to a four-year institution is essentially similar to a student who moves from high school to college. Many programs of financial aid information and guidance that were developed for use with secondary schools can be used effectively in community colleges.

However, in other ways transfer students are markedly different from those who enroll directly from high school. Generally transfer students from community colleges are older and more mature, and usually have better estimates of their financial needs. At the same time, they are more likely to have families of their own and therefore considerably more complicated financial situations.

A community college transfer student frequently comes with better developed job skills. If family obligations do not make it impossible, part-time work can play a more important part in the aid package for a transfer student. Previous borrowing may make it necessary to reduce the proportion of the package that typically would come from loans. Finally, because a community college transfer student may experience academic and environmental adjustment problems similar to those of a student entering directly from high school, self-help expectations normally made of upper-division students may have to be adjusted.

Talent Search and Educational Information Agencies

As postsecondary education has become increasingly involved in activities designed to find individuals outside of the traditional age population who can benefit from further education or training, there have developed an increasingly large number of agencies in the community responsible for providing information about the opportunities available and the supportive services that can make those opportunities realistic to low-income people, to adults seeking to upgrade their skills, or to those who find it necessary to retrain for new careers at midlife. For many of these individuals, financial aid is the most important supportive service that can be provided.

Personnel of these programs look to the postsecondary institutions for assistance in providing information about specialized services like student aid. In some instances the information needed is provided by special program offices at the institution. In other instances the aid office must be prepared to provide it directly. Some of the information provided to and through high schools and community colleges may suffice; other information may need to be specially prepared for the individuals served by these community agencies.

Sponsors of Student Aid Programs

In the early days of the modern era of student aid administration, most resources came from private donors, organizations, and business firms. Responsibility for securing additional student aid funds typically was assigned to a development office or to the office of alumni affairs. The role of the aid administrator typically was passive, assisting those other offices in their communications with individuals and organizations who were or who might become benefactors of the institution.

Private donors and sponsors of aid programs can continue to be a major source of support for students at all kinds of institutions, and the aid administrator can provide the offices responsible for their cultivation with advice on the best way to make grant or loan funds available to the institution to assist students in meeting costs. In addition to personal assistance, the aid administrator can help by providing copies of reports on the activities of the office: the amount of aid funds available in the various programs, the characteristics of all students who applied for aid as well as those who were assisted, the amounts of aid that were awarded and the forms — grants, loans, jobs — in which it was offered, and the amounts of unmet need of those whose applications were denied. This kind of information can be used by the development officer to interest potential sponsors and donors in the needs of particular kinds of students at the institution.

The massive growth of the federal and state governments' involvement in the area of financial aid, however, has placed the aid administrator in a much more direct and much more important role in the development of student aid resources at the institution. At most institutions, the aid administrator "develops" as much or more resources than do either the development officer or the director of alumni affairs.

Federal student aid, which has grown in appropriations 262 percent per full-time equivalent student during the period 1967 to 1976,[46] comes to the institution as a direct result of an application submitted, typically, by the director of financial aid. Before 1978, the amount of that federal aid was generally directly related to the ability of the aid administrator to complete the federal application. Changes in the application procedure that are being gradually introduced reduce the importance of "grantspersonship" in the determination of an institution's share of federal student aid allocations, but the aid administrator still has the responsibility for determining and documenting the needs of present and potential students at the institution. In many instances this documentation can be derived directly from the aid application files; in other instances it will require outreach and research on the part of the aid administrator to develop information about the needs of populations of students not currently being served, or being ill-served, by the present allocation of federal student aid.

In addition to the development of specific requests for federal support of students, the aid administrator should develop a more general role of advocacy and intervention as federal student aid policies, practices, and procedures are being developed. The purpose of publication of "Notices of Proposed Rule-making" in the *Federal Register* is to provide an opportunity for the broader community of informed individuals to contribute to the development of programs best suited to the needs of those most directly affected by them. In the area of student aid, the professional aid administrator is perhaps the most qualified to comment on these matters. In some instances it may also be appropriate for the aid administrator to mobilize students for the purpose of commenting on proposed or present changes. Even if direct political action may not be appropriate because of institutional policy or inclination, nothing should prohibit the aid office from posting the name and local office address and telephone number of elected officials who could be interested in taking action to redress grievances of voting-age constituents. The aid office can also support the activities of student organizations and student lobbies working to develop or modify student aid resources.

State student aid programs frequently offer more direct opportunities for participation on the part of institutional aid administrative personnel. Most have advisory committees that assist in the development of program policies and procedures. Many provide mechanisms for the participation of institutional representatives in the selection of recipients or the determination of stipends through "need analysis teams" working as paid or unpaid consultants to the state program. State programs may also provide opportunities for lobbying at more manageable levels than is true with the federal legislators. State representatives may call on individual aid administrators as expert spokespersons in the development of aid-program legislation.

The Federally Insured (Guaranteed) Student Loan Program requires that the financial aid office assist banks, commercial lending organizations, and loan guarantee agencies in certifying the eligibility of students and parents for loans to meet the expenses of education. It is important for the director of aid to develop sound working relations with agencies, particularly local banks, that are the source of substantial amounts of loan money for students.

The director of aid may be asked by such groups as labor unions, church organizations, and civic groups to aid them when they select students to receive financial assistance. Even though the applicants for these programs may not enroll in the local institution, the director of aid should help these groups to select the most deserving candidates. Not only is this help likely to be reciprocated by financial aid administrators in other communities, but a generous offering of professional assistance may encourage groups to make financial donations to the local educational institution.

Professional Colleagues

The growing importance of the role of student assistance programs in higher education generally makes it incumbent upon the director of aid to consult frequently, freely, and openly with colleagues in other institutions in order to strengthen services to students. The development of aid programs can be improved through active participation in meetings of "segmental" associations of institutional aid administrators (e.g., from all the private institutions in region or state); state and regional associations of student financial aid administrators (as well as in substate groups that have been organized in some areas); the National Association of Student Financial Aid Administrators; the College Scholarship Service Assembly (nationally and by region); and other related professional associations such as the American College Personnel Association, the National Association of Student Personnel Administrators, or the National Association of College and University Business Officers. Through these and other organizations devoted to the professional development of student support programs, the combined wisdom of many experts can be brought to bear on local and national problems.

Another method of participation is through submitting materials to the *Journal of Student Financial Aid*. The *Journal* has become the major mechanism for communicating professional developments, program innovations, and research results among the profession and to others interested in the activities of aid administrators. Recent editorial comments indicate that the *Journal* has not been overwhelmed with submissions. More aid administrators should make it the vehicle for sharing with colleagues.

The aid director and staff should be prepared to assist and to advise those who represent the institution at meetings of various professional organizations. For example, this assistance should be available to the college president as he participates in the work of the American Council on Education, to the registrar and admissions officers as they work with such groups as the American Association of Collegiate Registrars and Admissions Officers and the National Association of College Admissions Counselors, and to the faculty as they prepare to attend meetings of the societies that represent their several disciplines. The director of aid must become the source to which all members of the college staff and faculty may and will turn for information and advice on student financial aid matters.

Some Common Problems

The actual administrative problems and issues that each aid office must address will be rooted in the environment within which it must function. As noted earlier, institutional mission will in some measure dictate what the aid office does and the way in which it works. Available resources, both in amount and kind, will influence office activities and solve or create differing problems. Some state programs require little involvement from the individual campuses; others require major portions of time and attention. The administration of aid at a developing institution with increasing enrollment will be different from that at an institution facing potentially sharp declines in its traditional student population. But regardless of these differences, there are some issues and concerns that appear common to all student aid offices.

Document Control

The two previous editions of this booklet considered at length the desirability of the development and use of a single application for all forms of aid administered at an institution. That goal seems to have been achieved at nearly all institutions due, in large measure, to the influence of the federal government and the centralization of aid administration in a single office at most institutions. Yet the problems of document control seem to have grown, mainly because of the number of documents that must now accompany an aid application as it works its way through the process of evaluation, allocation, distribution, and collection.

Some institutions consider the Financial Aid Form (FAF) of the College Scholarship Service or the Family Financial Statement (FFS) of the American College Testing Program as their institutional application for aid. Most, however, supplement the need analysis document with an additional application that collects more complete demographic and nonfinancial data about students and their families. So for most institutions, the basic "application" consists of a personal data form, the need analysis document, any supplementary data provided (or required) for verification of the family's financial circumstances, and the need analysis report.

For undergraduate students, most institutions will also require a copy of the Basic Grant program's Student Eligibility Report (SER). Many also require that students apply for a state scholarship or grant before they will be considered for institutionally administered aid, and submit a copy of the appropriate state application form or award or denial notice. Transfer students are required also to document the aid received at all institutions previously attended.

Aid office staff members review these data, evaluate need and eligibility, and produce an award or denial notice. This is followed by a statement from the student accepting, modifying, or rejecting the offered assistance; an affidavit of educational purpose for federal aid recipients; disbursement schedules; promissory notes; and all the other institutional, state, and federal documents required to disburse the aid. Thus, even though the single application has become a common practice at most institutions, a completed student application file contains a number of documents.

One document that frequently is not present, however, is a master record on which the staff can indicate receipt of each document required to complete application, to document eligibility, and to authorize disbursal of aid. A master record is something that every institution should develop and include in each student's file. Some institutions have found it efficient to have that master record printed on the file folders — making it a permanent part of the folder, impossible to lose. Routine use of such a master record will assure an aid administrator that all required documents have been received and are part of a student's master file.

In addition to verifying that all the required documents are present in a student's file, an aid administrator must be certain that they have been treated or evaluated correctly. This represents the "qualitative" side of document control. The National Association of Student Financial Aid Administrators makes available a "Checklist for Review of Student Financial Aid Files" that can be used in reviewing student records to assure qualitative completeness. This checklist can provide an aid administrator with a means of conducting a self-audit of the adequacy of the office's record keeping and analysis practices. The checklist briefly reviews the documents that should be present in a student file and deals extensively with what qualifies as correct analysis and use of those documents.

Data Processing

For many years, data processing systems were much discussed but little implemented in support of financial aid administration. Some administrators expressed the belief that a data processing system would "dehumanize" their activities. Others believed that a computer could never match the "sensitivity" with which they constructed individual student aid packages. But most administrators at moderately sized institutions saw computers as a means of achieving better control, improving processing time, and providing a mechanism by which, "with routine tasks being handled by the computer, the professional staff can deal more effectively with the problems of individual students."[47] The decade of the 1970s has brought major increases in the use of automatic data processing systems in the financial aid office.

Unfortunately, many aid directors have attempted to implement data processing systems as a means of solving administrative problems caused by their manual clerical operations, rather than solving the clerical problems and then implementing a data processing system. The results frequently paralleled those of commercial firms that implemented data processing systems for similar reasons: "a computer can make a sick business look terminally ill. If there isn't an ordered and well-oiled set of procedures—however informal—to your business, wait. . . ."[48] In other cases, the aid administrator had not thought through completely what a data processing system was to do for the office and the institution and found that "if you don't know what you're going to do with the computer, it will do exactly what you have in mind—nothing!"[49]

In 1975, the College Scholarship Service sponsored the first of what was to become an annual series of invitational conferences on data processing in financial aid. Those conferences bring together financial aid and data processing administrators from institutions that have data processing systems and those who are seeking to implement them. For the former group the conferences provide an opportunity to compare problems and solutions and to find ways to improve their systems. The latter group of administrators are able to explore the options available for systems development and implementation.

Data processing systems for financial aid take a number of configurations, each appropriate to the institution and aid programs with which they must cope. They do, however, have generally common modules:[50]

1. *Application control.* Any system must keep track of data about the aid applicant population. This includes all the kinds of information described in the preceding section as well as the dates on which information was requested and received, and the action taken on the basis of that information.

2. *Need analysis and verification.* Most aid is based on financial need, and most data processing systems assist in some way in the performance of need analysis and verification of the data submitted for the determination of financial need.

3. *Packaging.* Some of the greatest time savings and increases in equitable treatment have come through the use of data processing systems to combine grants, loans, and work in consistent packages that implement institutional policies in a uniform way. At the same time, the packaging modules have proved to be among the most difficult for institutions to develop.

4. *Disbursing.* Most financial aid data processing systems provide some interface to the institution's accounting and business office systems to authorize the disbursement of aid according to schedules and procedures established jointly.

5. *Research and reporting.* Aid offices with data processing systems typically are much better able to meet reporting deadlines and to carry out research and evaluation activities because the information they need is more nearly accurate, accessible, and easily manipulated.

Many institutions have developed local systems that include some or all of these modules. Others have turned to outside sources and have adopted systems developed by others — other institutions, the College Board, or commercial data processing "software houses." The steps that an institution should follow in determining whether to automate and how to go about doing so, include:[51]

1. Prepare documentation of the current system, focusing on the problems that cause a need to upgrade and on opportunities for improved services or reduced costs that could be realized.

2. Define the resources that would be necessary to undertake an in-depth study of the problem and the development of recommendations, as well as the process that would be used to get from here to there.

3. Obtain management approval and financing for the conduct of the feasibility study.

4. Conduct the feasibility study.

5. Prepare a specific proposal for internal development of a system or implementation of an externally developed system.

6. If the decision is to build a new system specific to the institution, finalize systems specifications and design; design input documents and/or terminal data entry options, output documents, and reports; develop the actual computer programs and manual procedures; and prepare documentation.

7. If the decision is to implement an externally developed system, obtain and carefully review all documentation, computer programs, input and output documents; arrange for a

complete demonstration of the system; complete agreements to obtain or purchase the system; determine what modifications must be made to conform to local conditions; and document all modifications that are made.

8. Implement the system in a test environment and operate the system in parallel with prior procedures to assure full compliance with expectations.

9. Begin full independent operations. Review, evaluate, and modify the system as required at appropriate intervals.

In addition to the implementation of massive systems involved with substantially all aspects of the aid operation, many institutions are making increased use of sophisticated calculators for need analysis and word processing systems for the generation of award notices and other correspondence. These additional uses of technology further improve accuracy and reduce the amount of staff time consumed in repetitive clerical activities.

Operating Policies and Procedures Manual

Whether "computerized" or not, the practices and procedures of an institution's aid operation should be fully documented. This documentation should be included in a formal manual, available to all current staff as a reminder of how things should be and as a training device for newly hired staff.

In the spring of 1978, the National Association of College and University Business Officers cooperated with NASFAA in sponsoring a series of workshops on financial aid administration directed at business office personnel. In preparation for those workshops, the business officers were asked to complete self-evaluation check lists describing their beliefs about the adequacy of their institution's financial aid office. A tabulation of the responses showed that the business officers were most likely to rate their institutional aid office as inadequate in the area of documentation. The statement most frequently cited as "inadequate" was "current office policies and procedures manual."[52] The aid administrator can overcome that perception of inadequacy by developing and sharing a manual that includes descriptions of the following:

1. *The process of applying for aid.* Who may apply? What does one do to apply?

2. *Building and maintaining a student's file.* What data and documents are required? How are they requested? When is a file complete?

3. *Determination of eligibility.* Who decides and on what basis are budgets determined? Which students are dependent and which independent? Who decides how much is expected from parents and students? What are the eligibility criteria for each aid program?

4. *Packaging.* How are awards from different programs and types of funds combined? How are awards from noninstitutional sources considered? What flexibility do students have in accepting parts of the package?

5. *Notification and disbursement.* How are students and others informed of aid offered and accepted? When are disbursements made? How are institutional charges for tuition and fees, books and supplies, room and board, etc., handled?

6. *Review and revision.* Under what circumstances may awards be revised? How is verification performed? What are the standards for normal progress, and how are they enforced?

This brief listing sketches some of the contents of an institutional aid policy and procedures manual. Each institution should add material describing its own programs, interpretations that have been made of policies and procedures of federal and state programs, and other matters appropriate to a full description and understanding of the way in which the aid office and programs are actually operated.

The manual should also include an annual schedule of activities. Regular, recurring activities such as redesign of the application, printing annual supplies of forms, holding training sessions for staff and counselors, mailing renewal applications, preparing the Fiscal-Operations Report and Application to

Participate in Federal Student Financial Aid Programs (FISCAPP), etc., should be noted. The calendar should be up-dated weekly or monthly as nonrecurring activities are identified. It is particularly useful to keep the calendar up to date as a kind of "log" of office activities that can then be used as a planning tool for next year. Some activities that appear to be nonrecurring may in fact happen at about the same time each year but fail to be recorded.

The office calendar should be shared with all members of the staff and with personnel in other offices who are concerned with or dependent on the aid office. As updates occur they too should be shared. Knowledge of what is on the current agenda of the aid office may help others in planning activities that will support (or avoiding activities that would conflict with) those of the aid office. Modified versions of the calendar might be shared with the campus newspaper as a means of publicizing activities in which students could or should participate.

The NASFAA makes available to members a large wall calendar preprinted with the dates and locations of professional meetings, seminars, workshops, and conferences as well as deadlines common to most or all aid offices. This document is a good starting point for the development of a specific institutional operations calendar if one is not currently in use.

The manual might also include written descriptions of the jobs of the different personnel in the aid office. These descriptions should provide a full and complete statement of the actual duties discharged by each individual (or by each type of employee in a larger office), rather than serve as a device to justify a particular salary level (as is too frequently the case). Realistic job descriptions can help both new employees and personnel of other institutional offices understand how the aid office actually functions in carrying out its mission.

Student Consumer Information

Section 493A of the Education Amendments of 1976 specified a number of kinds of information that institutions must provide to students as a condition of their participation in federal student aid programs. At most institutions, the responsibility for providing this information was assigned to the financial aid office. At a number of institutions, however, the provision of required student consumerism information was integrated into a larger project of "better information for student choice" in a realization that "providing better information to students earlier, particularly about financial aid, would . . . presumably increase the number of colleges they considered and, perhaps, the likelihood that they would enroll."[53]

The kinds of information that students should have is the subject of considerable debate. A National Task Force on Better Information, supported for two years by the Fund for the Improvement of Postsecondary Education, made some preliminary recommendations.[54] A follow-up conference held at the University of Michigan brought together representatives of a number of different academic disciplines, students, and legislators to help develop a "do-able" list. The recommendations of that conference suggested that, as a condition of participation in the federal student aid programs, institutions be required to provide materials that accurately describe the following:

a. The student financial assistance programs available to students who enroll at the institution;

b. Statements, tables, or examples that permit a student to determine the probability of financial aid and likely net cost after probable grant assistance that must be paid by students of similar family income, dependency, and housing status;

c. The procedures by which students should apply for financial assistance;

d. The rights and responsibilities of students receiving financial assistance;

e. A description of the tuition, room, board, and other usual charges as well as a statement of policy concerning refunds for prepaid charges if the student, with proper notification, terminates the course of study prior to its scheduled completion;

f. The names of associations, agencies, or governmental bodies which accredit, approve, or license the institution and its programs, and a statement of what that accreditation, approval, or licensing implies;

g. The likelihood of its credits being accepted upon transfer to another institution, and by what kinds of institutions transfer credit may be granted;

h. Probable or possible limitations upon the employability of graduates, or their ability to sit for licensing or other examinations for any occupation or profession for which training is offered;

i. Significant, known, pending changes in the institution's admission or completion requirements, curricula, staffing, facilities, or costs;

j. The standards that students must maintain to remain eligible for continued attendance at the institution or in a particular program of study;

k. The names of programs or curriculums into which entry may be limited by facilities, staff, or admissions requirements that differ significantly from those generally applicable to the institution; and

l. The procedures by which students who believe they have been unfairly treated may pursue and appeal their grievances and the name and address of the individual to whom that appeal should be made.[55]

It seems likely that the Congressional reauthorization debates in 1979 and 1980 will expand, rather than contract, the information institutions are required to provide to students as a consequence of participation in federal student aid programs. If the ultimate federal requirements are as extensive as this list suggests they might become, the financial aid administrator may well be at the center of a large information development and dissemination program about the institution. The report of the National Task Force on Better Information provides a number of valuable suggestions about how that broader effort might be organized and conducted, as summarized in the following figure:[56]

Steps in Developing Better Information

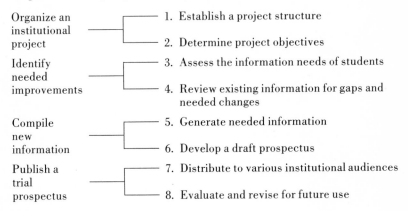

Organize an institutional project	1. Establish a project structure
	2. Determine project objectives
Identify needed improvements	3. Assess the information needs of students
	4. Review existing information for gaps and needed changes
Compile new information	5. Generate needed information
	6. Develop a draft prospectus
Publish a trial prospectus	7. Distribute to various institutional audiences
	8. Evaluate and revise for future use

A College Board booklet, *Making it Count,* describes a number of specific institutional efforts at providing better information to students in the particular area of costs and available financial aid. These projects, as well as those of the National Task Force, demonstrated that "better communication is possible, and actually serves the best interest of the institution."[57] Aid administrators who have become deeply involved in various better information projects have found them to be an enjoyable way to contribute to the needs of both students and their institutions.

One valuable resource in the development of better information is the Better Information Project: Prizes in Education (BIPPE), conducted by the National Student Educational Fund.[58] The BIPPE contest brings together large numbers of student-submitted information projects in a national competition. Copies of those judged to be best are distributed on request. Another source of information and assistance is Project CHOICE, the Center for Helping Organizations Improve Choice in Education, at the University of Michigan. Project CHOICE is organized to "assist institutions in responding to a variety of external pressures for more 'consumer-oriented' information about academic programs, financial aid availability, policies and procedures, and what currently enrolled students say about life on campus."[59]

Research

The practices and procedures of student aid administration have been developed in the almost complete absence of hard data and research supporting or refuting them. The literature is replete with articles reporting on "how we do it at old Siwash" and "wouldn't it be nice if. . . ." Very few articles include statements such as "the data demonstrate that . . ." or "examination of the performance of students who received . . . awards showed that they . . . ." There is a nearly complete lack of investigation of the impact of aid practices on students, institutions, and society. Even though the federal government has loaned billions of dollars to students since 1958, the literature of financial aid includes only one article describing the impact of borrowing on the postgraduate activities of recipients.[60]

The reasons for this lack of research are many. Some relate to the lack of training in research on the part of the aid administrator. As noted earlier, the NASFAA study showed that only 5 percent of responding aid directors held the doctorate degree, where research training typically occurs. Some relate to a lack of concern with research as one of the functions of the aid office. Only about 30 percent of the directors of aid responding to the NASFAA survey indicated that their office had conducted any research during the last two years. Fewer than half of those said that their research employed any test of statistical significance.[61] Other reasons undoubtedly relate to a lack of financial support by institutions for research in the financial aid office. Some must also relate to a lack of ideas about what can or should be the subject of research.

The kinds of research that can be most easily performed in the financial aid office and can most directly result in an impact on student aid administration has to do with policies. Policy research is research designed for the world of action rather than research designed to provide scholarly information about the subject of a particular academic discipline. The product of this kind of research is not necessarily an original contribution to the body of knowledge, but, rather, the product is action taken on the basis of information provided.

The "ten rules for policy research" developed by Nelson[62] apply well to the area of financial aid research:

1. *Know what's needed.* Identify the problem you are trying to solve and the goal you are trying to reach. Try to separate the essentials from the "wouldn't it be nice to know" kinds of questions. Break down the complex questions into simple ones.

2. *Don't wait to be asked.* The effective administrator needs to anticipate the important issues that will arise and to be slightly ahead of them. Partial information at the time it is needed is much better than complete information after the issue has been decided.

3. *Do it for more than one purpose.* When putting together information for a committee or a report to a sponsor, plan to use selected parts for memoranda to the president or others on campus who would be interested in the findings and look for ways to share it with colleagues in letters, speeches, or articles.

4. *Use what you've got in the desk drawer first.* This is the corollary of rule 3 — making use of the results of work that you have already done.

5. *Take advantage of what others have done.* Look for the experience of others in answering questions at your institution.

Take advantage of potential collaborators and existing resources in addressing policy questions.

6. *Keep it simple.* Abstract small bits of information that can be easily communicated to others who are involved in policy decisions and actions. One page memoranda addressing a single issue and offering to provide more detailed information may gain more attention than a 30-page report.

7. *It is not necessary to use fancy statistics.* For most audiences, statistics are not easily understood and often tend to discourage potential users from reading reports.

8. *Do it.* Research takes discipline. Perhaps the most difficult part of a financial aid research activity is simply starting it.

9. *The more you do it, the easier it gets.* The same names appear time and time again among lists of authors in financial aid. Few of those named are professional researchers — they are generally administrators who have produced one article, found it easy, and started on a second, third, fourth . . . .

10. *Fight for change with what you know.* Policy research can and most often should present and support a position. Advocacy and action are legitimate goals.

An aid office should have developed a "research agenda" listing the kinds of questions that might be addressed. Sharing such a list with the advisers of graduate students in disciplines like economics, accounting, social work, and sociology might produce some willing workers (who might qualify for work-study employment). They could be interested in satisfying personal educational needs while answering some of the questions of concern to the financial aid administrator and the institution.

Planning and Budgeting

The financial aid administrator needs to develop financial plans and budgets reflecting some very sophisticated forecasting and simulation activities.

The federal government is the largest supplier of financial aid for most institutions, but the amounts of allocations from the federal government frequently are not known at the time an institution wishes to make its initial offers of assistance to entering students. Further complicating the predictability of federal student aid are the frequent changes in the rules and regulations for determining eligibility and award amount. This is a particular problem with the Basic Grant program, where eligibility and award amount are determined largely independent of the institution. Changes in the "family contribution schedule" annually approved by Congress comparably change student eligibility.

Changes in the level of funding for programs, both federal and state, also require an aid administrator to modify institutional practice. As more, or less, money is available to students at the institution, the aid administrator needs to experiment with alternative methods of allocating the resources to best meet the needs of all students. Within that process care needs to be exercised to assure that students in groups of particular concern to the institution are not unfairly treated. The aid administrator also needs to make plans to reflect changes in institutional charges and costs in student aid eligibility and awards.

An additional planning need of the financial aid administrator is to develop the operating budget for the office. This involves both prediction of the number of items that will be required—from paper clips to typewriters—and estimation of how much those items will cost some time in the future. Without an adequate level of operating funds even the right amount of available student aid will be difficult to disburse.

Many institutions have developed or purchased data processing systems with the capability of performing these kinds of simulations. In addition to making financial plans, these kinds of systems provide an institution with the ability to "model" the impact of alternative proposals for change in student aid eligibility (or postage rates) in order to anticipate their needs.

These institutions are also in a position to comment on the effect of possible changes with specific data about their impact on students and the institution. Such information frequently influences the direction of changes made by outside agencies. It can also influence institutional decisions. Knowledge of how much of a proposed tuition increase would have to be returned in the form of student aid in order to maintain parity can be persuasive to the institutional administration considering such changes.

Without such data processing systems, the planning and budgeting tasks of the aid office are more complicated. A powerful desk calculator and a knowledge of forecasting techniques such as are taught in business economics and statistics courses can facilitate the process. It remains, however, a complicated and cumbersome exercise when done manually.

Summary

This chapter has identified a few of the areas in which solutions to problems separate the "model" college financial aid office from the average. Reality suggests that many of these problems will remain unsolved for a substantial number of institutions for the foreseeable future in the absence of adequate funding for research and development activities in financial aid. Perhaps one seminal characteristic of the model financial aid office is the recognition it receives from senior administration at the institution and the financial support that administration provides to the solution of the issues and concerns described here. The development of that level of recognition is one of the most important tasks of the financial aid administrator.

References

1. Merle Curti and Roderick Nash, *Philanthropy in the Shaping of American Higher Education.* New Brunswick, N.J.: Rutgers University Press, 1965, p. 7.
2. *Higher Education and National Affairs,* Vol. XXVIII, No. 4, January 26, 1979, p. 2.
3. Estimated from *Federal Aid to Postsecondary Students: Tax Allowances and Alternative Subsidies.* Washington, D.C.: Congressional Budget Office, 1978, p. 5.
4. Joseph D. Boyd and Sybil E. Francis, *National Association of State Scholarship and Grant Programs 10th Annual Survey, 1978-79.* Deerfield, Il.: NASSGP, 1979.
5. Cash Kowalski, *The Impact of College on Persisting and Non-Persisting Students.* New York: Philosophical Library, 1977, p. 83.
6. Robert E. Stoltz, *Financial Aid Report,* March 1973.
7. George Nash and Paul F. Lazarsfeld, *New Administrator on Campus: A Study of the Director of Financial Aid.* New York: Bureau of Applied Social Research, Columbia University, 1968.
8. National Association of Student Financial Aid Administrators, *Characteristics and Attitudes of the Financial Aid Administrator.* Washington, D.C.: NASFAA, 1978, p. 16.
9. NASFAA, *Characteristics of Aid Administrator,* p. 62.
10. Frederick Rudolph, *The American College and University.* New York: Alfred A. Knopf, Inc., 1962, p. 177.
11. Frederick Rudolph, "Myths and Realities of Student Aid," *College Board Review,* No. 48, Fall 1962, pp. 18-23.
12. Ibid.
13. Ibid.
14. John F. Morse, "Interview," *U.S. News & World Report,* Vol. XLVII, No. 5, February 1, 1960, pp. 79-83.
15. Education Amendments of 1972, enacted June 23, 1972. P.L. 92-318, Sec. 131 (b) (1). 86 Stat. 251, 252.
16. Rudolph, *American College,* p. 177.
17. A. G. Sidar and David P. Potter, *No Need/Merit Awards—A Survey of Their Use at Four-Year Public and Private Colleges and Universities.* New York: College Entrance Examination Board, 1978, p. 6.
18. Gregory A. Jackson, "Financial Aid and Student Enrollment," *Journal of Higher Education,* 1978, Vol. 49, No. 6, pp. 548-549.
19. Sidar and Potter, *No Need/Merit Awards,* p. 9.

20. William D. Van Dusen, *The Coming Crisis in Student Aid*. New York: The Aspen Institute for Humanistic Studies, 1979, p. 6.

21. Morton A. Rauh, *Standardization of Financial Data*. Address presented at the Annual Meeting of the College Scholarship Service, New York, N.Y., October 25, 1966.

22. James L. Bowman and D. Bruce Johnstone, "Loans to Parents: New Help for the Middle-Income Family," *College Board Review*, No. 98, Winter 1975-76, pp. 24-30.

23. Editorial, *Los Angeles Times*, Tuesday, February 27, 1979.

24. The NASFAA "Statement of Good Practices" closely parallels the CSS statement of practices and is included in the *National Membership Directory* available from the NASFAA's Washington, D.C., office.

25. Warren W. Willingham, *Professional Development of Financial Aid Officers*. Palo Alto, Ca.: College Entrance Examination Board, 1970.

26. NASFAA, *Characteristics of Aid Administrator*, pp. 14-15.

27. Archie R. Ayers, Phillip A. Tripp, and John H. Russell, *Student Services Administration in Higher Education* (OE-53026). Washington, D.C.: United States Department of Health, Education, and Welfare, 1966.

28. Nash and Lazarsfeld, *New Administrator*.

29. NASFAA, *Characteristics of Aid Administrator*, pp. 104-105.

30. Ibid.

31. Panel on Student Financial Need Analysis, *New Approaches to Student Financial Aid*. New York: College Entrance Examination Board, 1971.

32. Memorandum from the NASFAA Committee on Program Review, November 19, 1977.

33. Nash and Lazarsfeld, *New Administrator*.

34. Robert J. Kates, Jr., James E. Nelson, and William D. Van Dusen, *The Staffing of Financial Aid Offices: Some Facts and Observations*. New York: College Entrance Examination Board, 1978.

35. The National Association of College and University Business Officers, *Accounting, Recordkeeping, and Reporting by Colleges and Universities for Federally-Funded Student Financial Aid Programs*. Washington, D.C.: NACUBO, 1972, p. i.

36. Kates, Nelson, and Van Dusen, *Staffing of Aid Offices*, p. 8.

37. Edward Sanders, "The New Admissions Scene," *College Board Review*, No. 87, Spring 1973, p. 30.

38. NASFAA, *Characteristics of Aid Administrator*, pp. 29-31.

39. K. E. Farber, U. E. Landauer, R. F. Mensel, and S. Sokatch, *1978-79 Administrative Compensation Survey*. Washington, D.C.: College & University Personnel Association, March 1979, pp. 11-13.

40. NASFAA, *Characteristics of Aid Administrator*, p. 18.

41. Nash and Lazarsfeld, *New Administrator*.

42. NASFAA, *Characteristics of Aid Administrator*, p. 22.

43. *Selective Admissions in Higher Education: A Report of the Carnegie Council on Policy Studies in Higher Education.* San Francisco, Ca.: Jossey-Bass, Inc., 1977, p. 76.
44. *Administration of Student Financial Aid in the Oregon State System of Higher Education.* Salem, Or.: Oregon Educational Coordinating Commission, 1978, p. 20.
45. Christopher Jencks, "Social Stratification and Higher Education," in *Financing Higher Education: Alternatives for the Federal Government,* M. D. Orwig, editor. Iowa City: American College Testing Program, 1971, p. 78.
46. *Federal Aid to Postsecondary Students,* p. 13.
47. William Rodgers, *Data Management.* Iowa City: American College Testing Program, 1978, p. 3.
48. Christopher D. Kloek, *Winning the Computer Game.* Santa Barbara, Ca.: DDC Publications, 1978, p. 5.
49. Ibid.
50. Modified from William D. Van Dusen, Hal F. Higginbotham, and Edmund C. Jacobson, *The Asilomar Guide to Implementing Financial Aid Data Processing Systems.* To be published by the College Board.
51. Ibid.
52. Unpublished analysis of check lists collected by Mrs. Gene Miller, Director of Financial Aids, Pasadena City College, Pasadena, Ca.
53. Jackson, "Financial Aid," p. 571.
54. *Better Information for Student Choice: Report of a National Task Force.* Washington, D.C.: American Association for Higher Education, 1978, 62 pp.
55. Recommendations of the Ad Hoc Committee on Student Consumer Information reported in *Legislative Recommendations for Reauthorization of the Higher Education Act and Related Measures.* Washington, D.C.: United States House of Representatives Committee on Education and Labor, March 1979, Appendix, pp. 50-55.
56. *Better Information for Student Choice,* p. 33.
57. *Making it Count: A Report on a Project to Provide Better Financial Aid Information to Students.* New York: College Entrance Examination Board, 1977, p. 21.
58. *Resources Brochure.* Washington, D.C.: National Student Educational Fund.
59. *Choice Comments,* Vol. 1, No. 1, February 1978, p. 1.
60. Jerry S. Davis and William D. Van Dusen, *Guide to the Literature of Student Financial Aid.* New York: College Entrance Examination Board, 1978.

61. NASFAA, *Characteristics of Administrator*, p. 147.
62. James E. Nelson, *Research that I Can and Should Do*. Address presented at the Annual Meeting of the College Board, New York, October 1978.